FROMMER'S TOURING GUIDES

AMSTERDAM

Ms. Susan Baker
2300 Phoenix Hill Dr
Louisville, KY 40207-1227

Author: **Hélène and Pierre Willemart**
Translation: **Alister Kershaw**
Additional text: **Gila Walker**
Editor: **Lisa Davidson-Petty**
Photo credits: **Diaf:** J.P. Langeland, pp. 23, 28, 32, 41, 123;
B. Simmons, p. 59 – **Explorer:** S. Grandadam, p. 114 – **J. Hureau,** p. 75 – **Phototheque:** R. Decker, pp. 52, 107; B. Trutmann, p. 103 – **S. Rasmussen,** pp. 12, 17, 36, 63, 71, 79, 83, 91, 98, 119.

This edition published in the United States and Canada in 1990 by Prentice Hall Press.
A division of Simon & Schuster Inc.
15 Columbus Circle.
New York, New York 10023.

ISBN 0-13-332314-5
ISSN 1042-8712

Printed in France by CLERC S.A. · 18200 Saint-Amand

FROMMER'S TOURING GUIDES

AMSTERDAM

PRENTICE HALL

NEW YORK   LONDON   TORONTO   SIDNEY
TOKYO   SINGAPORE

▰ HOW TO USE YOUR GUIDE

● Read the sections **'Planning Your Trip'** p. 15, **'Practical Information'** p. 19, **'Amsterdam in the Past'** p. 37 and **'Amsterdam Today'** p. 49 for background information.

● The rest of the guide is for use once you arrive. It is divided into **itineraries** and includes sections on museums and environs of Amsterdam.

● A section called **'Amsterdam Addresses'** is provided at the end of the guide, p. 117. It includes a selection of hotels, restaurants, cafés and shops.

● Use the **'Index'** p. 137 to locate a site, a person or practical information.

● A **'Useful Vocabulary'** section p. 129 provides a list of common Dutch words and phrases and useful terms for traveling, accommodation and restaurants.

● To locate recommended sites, hotels and restaurants on the maps, refer to the map coordinates printed in blue in the text. Example: I, B3.

▰ SYMBOLS USED

Sites, monuments, museums, points of interest
★★★ Exceptional
★★ Very interesting
★★ Interesting.

Hotels and restaurants
See p. 117 for an explanation of classifications.

▰ MAPS

Amsterdam I 8-9

Amsterdam II 10-11

Itinerary I 57

Itinerary II 69

Itinerary III 78

Itinerary IV 82

Rijksmuseum 86-87

▬ CONTENTS

Introduction to Amsterdam 13

Amsterdam in Brief 14

Planning Your Trip 15

When to go, 15 – Getting there, 15 – Entry formalities, 16 – Money, 17 – What to take, 18 – Before you leave: some useful addresses, 18.

Practical Information 19

Accommodation, 19 – Airlines, 19 – Business hours, 19 – Currency exchange, 20 – Electricity, 20 – Embassies and consulates, 21 – Emergencies, 21 – Entertainment, 21 – Festivals and public holidays, 22 – Food and drink, 24 – Getting around Amsterdam, 26 – Language, 29 – Media, 29 – Organizing your time, 30 – Post office, 31 – Safety precautions, 31 – Shopping, 31 – Sightseeing tours, 33 – Sports, 33 – Telephone, 34 – Time, 34 – Tipping. 34 – Tourist information. 35.

Amsterdam in the Past 37

Amsterdam Today 49

I – The Historic Heart of the City 55

The Dam, 55 – From the Damstraat to the Nieuwmarkt, 58 – From the Montelbaan Tower to the Weepers' Tower, 60 – Amstelkring, Oude Kerk and the red-light district, 62 – Around the Damrak, 64 – From the Kalverstraat to the Singel, 65.

II – The Golden Age 67

Around the Prinsengracht and Herengracht, 68 – The Fodor, Van Loon and Willet Holthuysen Museums, 69 – Around Waterlooplein, 72 – Rembrandt's House, 75.

III – North-west Amsterdam: The Jordaan . . . 77

The Jordaan, 77 – Prinseneiland and its warehouses, 80 – Herenmarkt and the colonial era, 80.

IV – The Amsterdam School of Architecture . . 81

De Dageraad Building Cooperative, 82 – Eigenhaard Building Cooperative, 83.

Museums of Amsterdam 85

Rijksmuseum, 85 – Van Gogh Museum, 89 – Stedelijk Museum, 93 – Historical Museum, 96 – Other Museums, 98.

Environs of Amsterdam 101

Monnickendam, 101 – Marken, 102 – Volendam, 104 – Edam, 105 – Haarlem, 107 – Muiden Castle, 113 – Naarden, 115.

Amsterdam Addresses 117

Useful Vocabulary 129

Suggested Reading 136

Index 137

INTRODUCTION
TO AMSTERDAM

Amsterdam is a hauntingly beautiful city. It has been a continual source of inspiration for artists, including Rembrandt and Van Gogh. More than 100 years ago, Van Gogh wrote a lovely description of the city at nightfall: 'the ground dark, the sky still lit by the glow of the setting sun, the row of houses and steeples against it, lights in the windows everywhere and the whole mirrored in the water.'

Amsterdam has changed, of course, but Van Gogh's description could have been written yesterday. The old gabled houses with their flat façades now sit alongside more modern constructions, but they still overlook the cobblestoned streets and canals in which they are reflected.

Walk through the streets of the city and look at the buildings, bridges and canals: the ever-changing light of each passing day and season is an extraordinarily pleasurable experience. No wonder this city is the fourth most popular tourist destination in Europe after Paris, London and Rome.

Amsterdam is, in some ways, an oversized village. You can walk from one end to the other in little more than an hour and in a single day the visitor can acquire a real sense of the city. Your knowledge of the capital will deepen with a lengthier stay, but your initial impression will probably only be reinforced.

Simultaneously, Amsterdam has everything that a big city can offer: great museums, theatres, cinemas, concert halls, department stores and more. Amsterdammers are cosmopolitan and often multilingual, able to switch among up to five different languages with disconcerting ease.

Lovely gabled townhouses line many of Amsterdam's canals.

Amsterdam in brief

Location: Amsterdam is located at the mouth of the IJ River, in the north-west area of the Netherlands.

Origin of the name: It comes from the Dutch word *amsteldam,* or dam of the Amstel River.

Political status: Capital of the Netherlands and part of the Randstad Holland district, which includes the country's four largest cities: Rotterdam, Utrecht, The Hague and Amsterdam.

Population: It is the largest urban centre of the Netherlands, with a population of close to 700,000 people in the city itself, and 945,000 including the suburbs.

Language: Dutch, although English and German are widely spoken.

Religion: 60% of the population are non-affiliated, 21% are Roman Catholic and 19% are Protestant.

Tourism: This is one of the major industries in Amsterdam, which accommodates 2.2 million visitors per year. It is one of the largest historical centres in Europe, with some 7000 houses classified as historical monuments.

Other statistics: There are 160 canals, 2100 bridges and close to 2000 houseboats. Amsterdam is a city of bicyclists; with 600,000 bicycles, there are two for every three people. There are 1400 cafés, and the 60 theatres and concert halls offer 14,000 performances each year – an average of 35 per day!

The unique atmosphere of Amsterdam is largely due to what the Dutch call *gezelligheid*. The word denotes a cozy, warm, sociable ambience. It is not only noticeable in the homes where the lace curtains of the living room are always open in traditional Dutch style. It is ever-present in the cafés and even in the streets of the city.

Amsterdammers cherish the *gezelligheid* of their city which, they fully realize, makes it a wonderful place to live in and a glorious place to visit.

PLANNING YOUR TRIP

▬ WHEN TO GO

Amsterdam is most beautiful in the spring when the whole city seems to be blossoming, with flowers in the parks, in the public gardens and on the windowsills. In summer, the tree-lined canals make Amsterdam one the greenest cities in Europe. Winds from the north can make the capital quite chilly in autumn and winter but the city retains its extraordinary beauty: the canals reflect the gilded leaves in the fall and the early morning mist covers the city. During the winter months, the fallen leaves reveal the façades of Amsterdam's patrician homes. During the height of the tourist season, in summer, make sure you reserve a hotel room at least a couple of weeks in advance.

Average temperature

	Jan min	Jan max	Mar min	Mar max	May min	May max	July min	July max	Sept min	Sept max	Nov min	Nov max
°F	32	39	34	46	44	61	54	68	50	66	39	43
°C	0	4	1	8	7	16	12	20	10	18	4	6

Average rainfall

	Jan	Mar	May	July	Sept	Nov
in/cm	2.5/6.4	1.9/4.9	2/5.2	3.1/8.1	2.6/6.8	3/7.7

▬ GETTING THERE

By plane

Amsterdam is easy to get to by air; airline companies offer direct flights from most major cities. These include: Air UK, British Airways, KLM, KLM Canadian Air, Northwest Orient Airlines, Pan Am, Qantas and TWA. Most of these companies have offices in major cities in Australia, Canada, Great Britain and the United States. You can call them directly or contact your travel agent for further information concerning flights and organized tours.

Airport

Flights arrive at Schiphol International Airport, 9.3 mi/15 km south-west of Amsterdam. There is a GWK exchange office *(Mon-Sat 8am-8pm, Sun 10am-4pm)* and a baggage-check service *(daily 6am-11pm; f1 per item)*. For arrival information: ☎ 601 0966, for scheduled flights, 511 0666 for charter flights.

You can get to the city centre by taxi (approximately f1.35), bus (n° 173) or train. Trains are the easiest and cheapest way to reach Amsterdam. The train service links Schiphol to the centre with trains every 15 minutes. The 20-minute ride costs f4.50. For train information, ☎ 23 8383 *(Mon-Fri 8am-10pm, Sun 9am-10pm)*.

By bus

Almost all buses arrive at Amsterdam's Centraal Station, in the heart of the city. From here, it is easy to take either a tram or bus to your destination.

By car

The Netherlands are fully integrated into the toll-free European road network. Once in the Netherlands, take highway A2 or A4 to get to Amsterdam and then simply follow the signs 'centruum' after leaving the highway. Visitors should be advised, however, that it is very difficult to park within the city, especially in the centre. You may find it more practical to leave your car at the hotel and tour the city by tram, bus or on foot. For parking information, see p. 27.

By train

The Dutch railway system offers a regular train service to more than 180 cities throughout Europe. Trains arrive at Amsterdam's Centraal Station.

▬ *ENTRY FORMALITIES*

Passport and visa

For a stay not exceeding three months, citizens of Australia, Canada, Great Britain, the United States and EEC countries do not need a visa. A valid passport is sufficient.

Health precautions

No vaccination of any kind is required for entry into the Netherlands.

Driving

Cars, motorbikes, scooters, trailers and caravans for private use do not require any customs papers. Motor vehicles must have a sticker indicating nationality. Drivers entering the Netherlands must possess a valid national (or international) driver's license and the car registration papers. Insurance is mandatory.

Customs

Visitors to the Netherlands are allowed to bring in 300 cigarettes, if they are bought in the EC, or 200 if purchased duty-free or outside the EC. A maximum of one litre of spirits (over 22° proof) is allowed, plus five litres of an alcoholic beverage (wine, champagne, etc.) under 22° proof.

Barges still travel on Amsterdam's intricate canal system.

There is no limit concerning currency import or export. Animals must have a valid certificate stating that they have been vaccinated against rabies. This vaccination must have been given at least 30 days before entering the Netherlands. For further information, apply to a veterinarian or the Dutch Embassy in your country.

▬ *MONEY*

The Dutch monetary unit is the *guilden,* or guilder, divided into 100 *centen*. To avoid confusion, visitors should know that although the Dutch will indicate a price by telling you five guilders, the written price is prefixed with an 'f' for florin. Example: f7 is seven guilders. Bank notes are issued in the following denominations: f5 (green), f10 (blue), f25 (red), f50 (yellow), f100 (brown), f250 (violet) and f1000 (green).

Credit cards

Most hotels, restaurants and stores accept internationally recognized credit cards (American Express, Diners Club, Eurocard, Mastercard and Visa) and travelers checks.

Budget

Your budget will obviously depend on the type of accommodation and eating places you select. A double room in a hotel will cost from 60 to 200 guilders. A light lunch will not be more than 15 guilders, while dinner can cost from 30 to 300 guilders.

■ WHAT TO TAKE

You will need warm clothing if you visit Amsterdam in the autumn or winter and light attire for the spring and summer. Bring along rainwear if you plan to come during the rainy season (August to November). A good pair of walking shoes is essential for Amsterdam's cobblestoned streets.

■ BEFORE YOU LEAVE: SOME USEFUL ADDRESSES

Netherlands Board of Tourism

Australia, Suite 302, 5 Elizabeth St., Sydney, NSW 2000, ☎ (2) 276 921.

Canada, Suite 710, 25 Adelaide St. E., Toronto, Ont. M5C 1Y2, ☎ (416) 363 1577.

Great Britain and **Ireland,** 25-28 Buckingham Gate, London SW1 E6LD, ☎ (01) 630 0451.

United States, 21st floor, 355 Lexington Ave., New York, NY 10017, ☎ (212) 370 7367; Suite 326, 225 N. Michigan Ave., Chicago, IL 60601, ☎ (312) 819 0300; Room 401, 605 Market St., San Francisco, CA 94105, ☎ (415) 543 6772.

Embassies

Australia, 130 Empire Circus, Yarralumla, Canberra ACT 2600, ☎ (62) 733 111.

Canada, 3rd floor, 275 Slater St., Ottawa, Ont. K1P 5H9, ☎ (613) 237 5030.

Great Britain, 38 Hyde Park Gate, London SW7, ☎ (01) 585 5080.

Ireland, 160 Merrion Rd., Dublin 4, ☎ (1) 693 444.

United States, 4200 Linnean Ave., Washington DC 20008, ☎ (202) 244 5300.

PRACTICAL INFORMATION

▬ ACCOMMODATION

See the section 'Amsterdam Addresses' p. 117 for specific hotel listings.

Amsterdam offers a wide range of hotels from luxury establishments to small hostels, but it can be hard to find rooms available, especially during peak tourist periods. It is a good idea to reserve in advance by contacting the **National Reserverings Centruum** (National Reservation Centre), P.O. Box 404, 2260 AK, Leidschendam, ☎ (070) 20 2500, telex: 33775 (reservations cannot be made by telephone).

If you are already in the Netherlands, you can reserve a hotel room through the **VVV Logiesservice** (reservation service of the national tourist organization) available at any local VVV office that displays the sign **I Nederland.** The most conveniently located VVV offices are those at Schiphol Airport and outside Centraal Station, I, A5.

Amsterdam also has several youth hostels, and there are campgrounds in the vicinity that are easily accessible from the city centre (see p. 119).

▬ AIRLINES

British Airways, Stadhouderskade 4, I, E2, ☎ 85 2211.
British Caledonian, Rokin 134, I, C4, ☎ 26 2440.
KLM Leidseplein 1, I, D2, ☎ 74 7747.
Northwest Airlines, Museum Plaza, Weteringschars 85 c, I, F3, ☎ 27 7141.
Pan Am, Leidseplein 31 c, I, D2, ☎ 26 2021.
Qantas Airways, Stadhouderskade 6, I, E2, ☎ 83 8081.
TWA, Singel 540, I, D4, ☎ 22 7671.
Schiphol Airport, ☎ 601 0966 for scheduled flights, 511 0666 for charter flights.

▬ BUSINESS HOURS

Shops usually open Monday to Friday 9am-6pm. Department stores are open Tuesday to Saturday 9am-6pm, Monday 1-6pm. Many stores remain open until 9pm on Thursday. Banks are open Monday to Friday 9am-3pm, post offices Monday to Friday 9am-5pm and pharmacies Monday to Friday 8am–5:30pm.

Some food stores have special licenses to stay open until midnight and on Sundays. Here you can buy a variety of groceries, including cheeses, wines, cold cuts and pastries. Prices tend to be higher than in regular stores. There are several shops conveniently located in the centre of town:

Balthus, Vijzelstraat 127, I, D4, ☎ 26 9069.

Big Bananas, Leidsestraat 76, I, D3, ☎ 27 1900.

Doorneveld AvondverKoop, De Clercqstraat 1, I, C1, ☎ 18 1727.

◼ CURRENCY EXCHANGE

Cash currency may be freely imported into the Netherlands or exported by non-residents. Currency, Eurocheques and travelers checks may be easily exchanged in banks or exchange offices. Banks *(open Mon-Fri 9am-4pm)* usually give the best rates. You can also change money at hotels, but the rates are generally not as good. The GWK exchange offices located throughout the city offer exchange rates equivalent to bank rates but the commission charge is slightly higher.

Banks

Algemere Bank, Vijzelstraat 68, I, D4, ☎ 29 9111; *open Mon-Fri 9am-4pm.*

American Express, Damrak 66, I, B4, ☎ 26 2042; *open Mon-Fri 9am-5pm, Sat 9am-noon.*

Verenidge Spaarbank, Singel 548, I, D4, ☎ 520 5911; *open Mon-Fri 9am-4pm.*

Ned. Middenstands Bank, Damrak 80, I, B4, ☎ 26 1271; *open Mon-Fri 9am-4pm.*

Exchange offices

GWK, Centraal Station, I, A5, ☎ 22 1324; *open Mon-Sat 7am-10:45pm, Sun 8am-10:45pm.*

Schiphol Airport, *open Mon-Sat 8am-8pm, Sun 10am-4pm.*

Change Express offices *(open daily 8am-midnight)*

● Damrak 17, I, A4, ☎ 24 6682.
● Kalverstraat 150, I, C4, ☎ 27 8087.
● Leidsestraat 106, I, D3, ☎ 22 1425.

Lost credit cards

American Express, ☎ 540 1919.

Diners, ☎ 557 3757.

MasterCard, ☎ (10) 457 0754.

Visa, ☎ 21 4621.

◼ ELECTRICITY

The electrical current everywhere in the Netherlands is 220 volts. Bring an adapter for electrical appliances such as hairdryers and portable irons that operate on 110 volts.

▬ *EMBASSIES AND CONSULATES*

Embassies (in The Hague)
Australia, Koninginnegracht 23, 2514 AB, ☎ (070) 63 0983.
Canada, Sophialaan 7, ☎ (070) 61 4111.
New Zealand, Mauritskade 25, 2514 HD, ☎ (070) 46 9324.

Consulates (in Amsterdam)
Great Britain, Koningslaan 44, II, D2, ☎ 76 4343.
United States, Museumplein 19, I, F2, ☎ 64 5661.

▬ *EMERGENCIES*

Foreign tourists are entitled to medical attention from the *Ziekenfonds* or **ANOZ** (medical insurance fund) if they are citizens of a country with which the Netherlands has signed an international convention or if they can provide the doctor, pharmacy or hospital with an international insurance form. For further information, contact ANOZ, Postbus 9069, 3506 GB Utrech, ☎ (030) 61 8881.

Hospitals
Academisch Medisch Centrum, Meibergdreef 9, ☎ 566 9111 (general) or 566 3333 (emergencies).
Onze Lieve Vrouwe Gasthuis, 1e Oosterparkstraat 179, II, D5, ☎ 599 9111.
Wilhemina Gasthuis, Eerste Helmerstraat 104, I, E1, ☎ 578 9111.

Useful telephone numbers
All-night pharmacies: 555 5277.
Ambulance: 555 5555.
Fire: 21 2121.
Medical assistance *(centrale doktersdienst):* 64 2111 or 79 1821.
Police: 22 2222.

▬ *ENTERTAINMENT*

Amsterdam has been one of the main cultural centres of Europe for centuries. During a single year, you can choose from among 15,000 performances in more than 50 theatres and concert halls. Seats for most plays, concerts, ballets and operas can be reserved through the **Amsterdam Uit Buro** (AUB), Leidseplein 26, I, D2, ☎ 21 1211. You can also reserve through all the major VVV offices (Amsterdam Tourist Bureau, see p. 35) located throughout the Netherlands.

Theatres
The theatre plays an important part in Amsterdam's artistic life. Theatres range from the **Stadsschouwburg,** Leidseplein 26, I, D2, ☎ 24 2311, a favourite of the Netherlands Dance Theatre, to the 100-year old **Theatre Carré,** Amstel 115-125, I, D5, ☎ 22 5225, a typical Amsterdam institution featuring pop music concerts, cabaret and ballet performances. Then there is the **Theatre de Engelbak,** Nes 71, I, B4, ☎ 24 3644 or 23 5723, with performances in both French and English, and

the **De Kleine Komedie,** Amstel 56, I, D5, ☎ 24 0534, where the repertoire is inspired by different aspects of life in Amsterdam.

Opera, Ballet and Dance

The **Muziektheater,** Waterlooplein 22, I, D5, ☎ 25 5455, has a new and impressive auditorium seating 1600 and is the home of the Netherlands Opera Company and the National Ballet Company.

Music

The **Concertgebouw,** Van Baerlestraat 98, I, F2, ☎ 71 8345, offers classical music performances by the world-renowned **Concertgebouworkest** and by pop music orchestras. **Sonesta Koepelzaal,** Kattengat 1, I, A4, ☎ 21 2233, is a former Protestant church where musical matinées are held.

Additional information is given in *Agenda,* a free monthly guide to cultural events, *Alert,* a monthly guide to current exhibitions and *Uit-Shop Leidseplein,* which gives details concerning all entertainment and booking information. These publications are available in bookshops and news-stands in Spui Square, I, C3, and at Centraal Station, I, A5. **VVV Amsterdam** also publishes *Amsterdam This Week* every Wednesday, which provides information on art and cultural events, restaurants and shopping (f0.75 in hotels and VVV offices).

If you are looking for other nighttime entertainment, you'll find numerous cabarets, nightclubs, bars, brasseries and restaurants around the Rembrandtsplein, I, D4, and the Leidseplein, I, D2, Amsterdam's equivalent of the Place Pigalle in Paris. See the section 'Amsterdam Addresses' p. 117 for a listing of nightclubs and discos.

▬ FESTIVALS AND PUBLIC HOLIDAYS

In addition to celebrations for religious and national holidays, Amsterdam holds numerous cultural festivals, especially during the summer. For a detailed listing of these events, apply to the **Uitburo** (see p. 21). The following holidays and festivals are of special interest to the tourist:

February

Carnival Parade: Held during the second or third week of the month, the parade starts at the **Oosterdok,** I, B5, and ends at **Rembrandtsplein,** I, D4. The cafés are even more cheerful than usual, with customers in costumes dancing and drinking.

March

Stille Omgang: On the Tuesday before Palm Sunday, thousands of Catholics make a pilgrimage to Amsterdam to join in a silent procession to the **Oude Kerk** (see p. 63) or to the *Heilige Stede* (the Holy Place). The procession commemorates a series of miracles believed to have taken place here in the mid-14th century. On the Tuesday preceding

Tulips and hyacinths, exported throughout the world, grace many of the most beautiful Dutch parks.

Palm Sunday in 1345, after receiving the Holy Sacrament from a priest, a dying man vomited and was revived. His vomit was swept up and thrown into the fire but the next day the Host was discovered in the burning coals. When the Host was retrieved, the red-hot coals caused no pain. Other miracles followed, including the repeated disappearance and reappearance of the Host and several miraculous healings. The next year the bishop declared the event to be a miracle and a chapel was built at the site.

April

Koninginnedag: The birthday of Queen Juliana (mother of the current queen, Beatrix) is celebrated on April 30. All day long and throughout the following night, Amsterdam's streets and cafés are filled with music and dancing. Children sell old toys, books and clothes, and there are all sorts of open-air performances. In honour of the queen, people wear orange scarves (orange is the royal family's colour) and drink *oranjebitter* (an orange-coloured liqueur).

June to August

Holland Festival: Opera, music, theatre and dance performances are held from June 1-30 in various theatres in Amsterdam and throughout the country.

Open Air Theatre: Free performances are given in **Vondelpark** throughout the summer.

September

Flower Parade: There is a magnificent floral procession from Aalsmeer to Amsterdam and back during the first week of September.

Jordaan Festival: For ten days, starting in the third week of the month, entertainment and cultural events are given in one of the liveliest sectors of the city.

November to December

St Nicholas Parade: Sometime during the second or third week of November, St Nicholas, the patron saint of Amsterdam, arrives at the docks to the sound of a gun-salute and the ringing bells of the St Nicholas church. Otherwise known as *Sinterklaas,* St Nicholas is the Dutch equivalent of Santa Claus. Each year he and his young servant Black Peter bring presents from Spain where they live the rest of the year. He parades on a white horse through the centre of the city while Black Peter throws handfuls of *pepernoten* (balls made of flour, sugar, anise, cinnamon and other spices) and cakes for the children.

St Nicholas Day: December 6 is St Nicholas' birthday. Helped by Black Peter, St Nicholas brings presents to good children. Older children and adults exchange presents which are often accompanied by long poems. It is traditional to eat *banketstaaf* (pastries filled with almond paste), gingerbreads, *pepernoten* and marzipan.

New Year's Eve: There are firework displays and dancing all over the city.

◼ FOOD AND DRINK

The old saying that 'you can eat in any language in Amsterdam' is no exaggeration. There are numerous Indonesian restaurants here as a result of the presence in Amsterdam of large communities from this former Dutch colony. Many Indonesian recipes and ingredients have become an integral part of Dutch cooking. You will also find French, Norwegian, Italian, Spanish, Hungarian, Greek, Japanese and other types of cuisine served in Amsterdam.

Dutch specialities

Dutch food is simple and substantial. A typical breakfast includes different kinds of bread, cheese, cold cuts, a medium-boiled egg, coffee or tea and milk. For lunch, the Dutch will add a salad or two to the above. Dinner consists of a filling soup, meat or fish often in the form of a stew, with potatoes, vegetables and a dessert such as custard or rice pudding.

If you want to have a quick lunch, try an *abelegde broodje* (a stuffed roll) or a *pannekoek* (a pancake served with either a savoury or sweet garnishing).

For dinner, sample the Dutch people's favourite soup: pea soup (*erwdnsoep* or *snert*) that should be thick enough for the spoon to stand upright. Typical stews include *stamppot,* potatoes, vegetables and meat; *boerenkool met worst,* kale, potatoes and smoked sausage; *zuurkool met spek,* sauerkraut, bacon, frankfurters and potatoes; *vijfschaft,* beans, carrots, onions, apples, potatoes and sausage; and *hutspot van kalfsborst,* breast of veal, bacon, vegetables and potatoes. Indonesian dishes, such as *nasi goreng* and *bami goreng,* baked rice or noodles with pieces of pork and shrimp, are served in both Indonesian and Dutch restaurants.

Dutch desserts tend to be as substantial as the meals. Try the *chocoladevla met mandarijntjes,* chocolate custard with mandarin oranges; *oliebollen,* doughnuts; or the various rice puddings and the gingerbread or spice cakes. Licorice, coffee-flavoured candies called *haagse hopjes* and *hagelslag,* chocolate vermicelli eaten on bread, are among the more popular Dutch sweets.

Dutch cheeses such as Edam and Gouda are world-renowned. Edam is a round yellow-orange cheese wrapped in a red rind. Gouda has a larger, flat form, a lighter colour and a stronger flavour. It can be bought either mild, mature or very mature: it becomes harder and has a more pronounced flavour as it ripens. Other less well-known cheeses include *leidse kaas,* seasoned with cumin seeds, and *friese nagelkaas,* seasoned with cloves.

Fish is plentiful in Holland. The two most popular fish are herring and eel, but you will also find plaice, sole, trout, crab, shrimp, oysters, mussels and more. The Dutch have been specialists in the preparation of herring since William Beukels discovered how to preserve them in 1384. Amsterdam boasts numerous *haringkar,* or herring stalls, where you can eat pickled, smoked or salted herring, and herring salads are on the menu of any restaurant serving regional food. Eels too are smoked and eaten hot on a slice of toast as an appetizer.

Restaurants

See the section 'Amsterdam Addresses' p. 117.

The main thing to remember is that most restaurants close at 10:30pm and some as early as 8:30pm. Since the best places are always full, it is a good idea to reserve ahead.

If you want to try Netherlands cuisine, watch for restaurants which display the *Netherlands Dis* sign. Wherever you see this sign, you can count on finding a genuine Dutch or regional speciality. More than 500 Amsterdam restaurants serve a tourist menu comprising an entrée, a main course and a dessert for f19.50. This price is standard everywhere although the meals themselves differ.

Drinks

Convivial drinking is a social institution in Amsterdam, and even a ritual. You will be reminded constantly that *jenever* is the world's first gin, invented in the Netherlands at the beginning of the 17th century. There are two types of Dutch gin: the light-yellow, strongly flavoured *oude* (old) and the younger, white *jonge*, which has a more neutral taste. There are rules about draught beer, or *Pilsje*, too: 'not lukewarm in the English way or cold in the American way' but at just the right temperature in the Amsterdam way.

Amsterdammers also relish *Kopstoot* (literally 'bang on the head'), in other words, beer and gin. You may also want to try *citroenjenever*, a lemon gin, or *bessenjenever*, a red currant gin.

Cafés and bars

See the section 'Amsterdam Addresses' p. 117.

Day or night, cafés offer an enjoyable experience. They often resemble huge living rooms filled with chairs and tables – sometimes including 'reading tables' on which newspapers and magazines are spread out. They remain animated and lively places well into the night.

Customers go to cafés to chat, to join up with neighbours or to meet with people from other areas. The 'brown café' is Amsterdam's answer to the London pub. Here the atmosphere is even more relaxed and easygoing. The floor may be hard-packed earth, and as the name indicates, everything has been stained brown from pipe and cigar smoke.

Amsterdammers have another 'institution' built round a cheerful drink, the *proeflokaal*, which literally means a 'testing place'. These places are filled with barrels, jars, bottles, earthenware pitchers and old curios. Customers come to gossip, meet their friends or simply have a snack in this warm 'brown' atmosphere, where the beers, wines and liqueurs mix with the smoke to create a special and unique feeling.

▬ GETTING AROUND AMSTERDAM

By bicycle

Bicycles are for rent all over the city, often at bicycle retailers or repair shops. You will usually have to pay a deposit of f50-200. Remember to take along your passport as proof of identity. The rates are approximately f6 per day and f24 per week. The following companies rent bicycles:

Damstraat Rent a Bike, Pieter Jacobsdwarsstraat 17, I, B4, ☎ 25 5029.

Fiets-O-Fiets, Amsterdamse Bos, entrance at Amstelveenseweg 880-900, II, F2, ☎ 44 5473.

Heja, Besteraerstraat 39, II, A2, ☎ 12 9211.

Koenders, Utrechtsedwarsstraat 105, I, E5, ☎ 23 4657.

Koenders Rent a Bike, Stationsplein Oostzijde, I, A5, ☎ 24 8391.

Stalling Amstel, Julianaplein 1, II, E5, ☎ 92 3584.

By boat

A tour of the canals (illuminated from April to October) will give you a unique glimpse of some of Amsterdam's most picturesque sites. It is the ideal introduction to the city. Numerous canal trips (one and a half hours) are organized by the following agencies:

Holland International, Prins Hendrikkade, opposite Centraal Station, I, C4, ☎ 22 7788.

Kooy, Oude Turfmarkt 125, I, C4, ☎ 23 3810.

Lovers, Prins Hendrikkade, I, A4, ☎ 22 2181.

Meyer's, Damrak Quays 4-5, I, A4, ☎ 23 4208.

Noord-Zuid, Stadhouderskade 25, I, E2, ☎ 79 1370.

Plas, Damrak, Quay 3, I, A4, ☎ 24 5406.

For an unusual experience, take a water taxi along the city's canals to your destination. This service was set up in 1988 and each gondola, as they are called, can take up to eight people. The taxis cost approximately f50 for 15 minutes, ☎ 75 0909.

By car

Drivers have a miserable time getting around the city because of the many bicycles and the lack of parking spaces. The best thing to do is leave your car in one of the parking lots (these are indicated by the letter P) on the Stadhouderskade which is near the museums, or on the Nassaukade or the Dam and then continue on foot. Incidentally, it is virtually impossible to park near any of the hotels in the centre of town.

Safety belts are compulsory in the Netherlands. As a general rule, vehicles coming from the right have priority. In built-up areas, the maximum speed limit is usually 30 mi/50 km per hour. Outside the city limits, the speed limit is 50 mi/80 km per hour on roads and 62 mi/100 km on highways. Yellow emergency telephones are provided on a number of highways. These are directly linked to the regional road safety centres.

Most international car rental companies have offices in Amsterdam or at Schiphol Airport.

Car rental

Avis, Nassau Kade, I, D2, ☎ 83 6061.

Budget, Overtoom 121, I, E1, ☎ 12 6066.

Europcar, Overtoom 51-53, I, E1, ☎ 18 4595.

Hertz, Overtoom 333, I, E1, ☎ 85 2441; Schiphol Airport, ☎ 17 0866.

Parking lots

Bijenkorf, Beursplein, I, B4.

Europarking, Marnixstraat 250, I, C2.

Krasnapolsky Hotel, St Jansstraat, I, B4.

Muziektheater, Waterlooplein, I, C5.

RAI, Europa Blvd., II, F4.

Bicycles, used by most Amsterdammers, come in all colours.

By pedalboat

This is a treat for the children while their parents visit museums! For f16.50 per hour for two people, you can pick up a pedalboat at one of the four landing docks: on the Singelgracht, I, F3, between the Rijksmuseum and the Heineken brewery; on the Prinsengracht, I, B2, near the Westerkerk church and the Anne Frank House; on the Keizergracht, I, D3, at the corner of Leidsestraat; and on the Leidseplein, I, E2, by the American Hotel. For further information, ☎ 26 5574; *open daily April through October, 9am-11pm.*

By tram, bus or subway

The public transport system is excellent and is a good way to explore the city. The tram system is the most extensive, with 16 lines and operates until about midnight; a network of eight night buses then provides transport until 4am, leaving Centraal Station for other areas in the city. The subway is fast and efficient but most of the stations are suburban, for commuter use. The main **GVB** (city transport) office is located in front of Centraal Station. Here you can obtain information, a free public transport map and an English-language guide to the ticket system.

An economical way to use the public transport is to buy a *dagkaart,* a ticket that allows you to travel on the trams, buses and subways for one or several days. This ticket costs f8,65 for one day and can be purchased in advance from a GVB office.

You can also buy a *strippenkaart,* which is valid throughout the Netherlands and can be purchased at the GVB offices, post offices or from ticket machines located in the subway stations. The most economical *strippenkaart* has 15 strips; 2-, 3- and 10-strip tickets can be purchased from the driver. You must cancel a certain number of strips per zone (two strips for one zone, three for two zones and so on) when you get on the bus, tram or subway.

Useful addresses

GVB offices (for tram, bus and subway information and tickets):

Stationsplein (in front of Centraal Station, I, A5), ☎ 27 2727; *open Mon-Fri, 7am-10:30pm, Sat, Sun 8am-10:30pm.*

Bulldog café, Leidseplein 15, I, D2; *open Mon-Fri, 8am-9:30pm, Sat, Sun 10am-5pm.*

Scheepvaathuis, Prins Hendrikkade 108-114, I, B5, ☎ 551 4977; *open Mon-Fri 7am-11pm.*

On foot

There is no better way of getting to know Amsterdam than on foot. It is made for pedestrians. The city centre is not large and the concentric canal system means that the distances between sites are never too great.

LANGUAGE (See 'Useful Vocabulary' p. 129)

You will find that English is widely spoken by most people you meet socially, by officials, in the more expensive hotels and restaurants and in many of the bigger stores. In other words, you should find it quite easy to get by in the main towns and there should be no trouble in dealing with transport and other officials.

Sometimes, however, it will be a great help to know a few words of Dutch, if only to recognize them when they are written. Dutch is an extremely hard language to speak and the Dutch are generally not accustomed to hearing foreigners attempt to speak their language.

The Useful Vocabulary section at the end of the guide lists some of the most common words; these will enable you to follow timetables, guidebooks, etc. It also includes a number of terms that occur in restaurant menus. Figures are more difficult, not to say impossible, for foreigners to understand. The best thing to do is to have them written down.

MEDIA

Newspapers

The main Netherlands newspapers are the *Volkskrant,* the *Telegraaf* (sensational news stories) and the *NRC-handelsblad* (equivalent to *The Times* of London).

Foreign newspapers and magazines can be bought at bookshops and news-stands in the centre of town, in big hotels, at the airport and at Centraal Station. All the major international newspapers are also available as well as English-language magazines listing entertainment and other events (*Amsterdam This Week, Agenda* and *Amsterdam Info*). A similar magazine, the *Uitkrant,* is available in theatres, bars and cinemas.

There are also several interesting art magazines published in English. *DAAT* (Dutch Art and Architecture Today) is a biannual publication on contemporary art and architecture in Holland. *Dutch Art,* put out by the Ministry of Cultural Affairs, contains interesting articles and interviews. *Makkom* and *Tableau* are bilingual magazines on the visual arts. *Zien Magazine* is devoted to contemporary Dutch photography, and *Wiederhall* to architecture. The bilingual *Kremlin Mole* contains interviews with poets and video artists, as well as reviews.

Radio

There are four channels: Radio 1 and Radio 2 concentrate on cultural programs, news and documentaries, Radio 3 is devoted to pop music and Radio 4 to classical music. You can also pick up BRT (Belgium), WDR (Germany) and the BBC (United Kingdom).

Television

The Netherlands has three television stations; two broadcast primarily in Dutch, while the third, Nederland 3, offers programs for foreign workers in Serbo-Croat, Arabic and Turkish.

You can also pick up the three German channels, the two Belgian channels, BBC 1 and BBC 2, English channels from the United Kingdom, and the French Channel 5, together with such other commercial channels as Sky Channel and Super Channel.

▬ ORGANIZING YOUR TIME

We have included two programs – a weekend and a five-day tour – which cover the essential sights in Amsterdam. For information on the Museum Pass, see p. 85.

Amsterdam in one weekend

First day

Morning: Itinerary I: Historic Heart of Amsterdam (see p. 55).
Afternoon: Canal trip (see p. 27).
Evening: Stroll through **the Jordaan** and dinner in one of the neighbourhood restaurants (see p. 77).

Second day

Morning: **Rijksmuseum** and **Van Gogh Museum** (see pp. 85, 89).
Afternoon: The **Anne Frank House** (see p. 68) and coffee in a brown café.
Evening: Dinner in a restaurant around **the Dam.**

Amsterdam in five days

First day

Morning: Itinerary I: Historic Heart of Amsterdam (see p. 55).
Afternoon: **Rembrandt's House** (see p. 75) and coffee in a brown café.
Evening: Try an Indonesian restaurant and the *rijsttafel* speciality, a selection of Indonesian dishes.

Second day

Morning: **Stedelijk** and **Van Gogh Museums** (see pp. 89, 93).

Afternoon: Canal trip (see p. 27).
Evening: Try a restaurant around **the Dam.**

Third day

Morning: Take a half-day excursion to **Marken** and **Volendam** (see p. 102).
Afternoon: Follow Itinerary II: The Golden Age (see p. 67).
Evening: Stroll and dinner around **Rembrandtsplein**.

Fourth day

Morning: **Rijksmuseum** (see p. 85).
Afternoon: Take an excursion to **Haarlem** and see the **Frans Hals Museum** (see p. 107).
Evening: Dinner in Haarlem.

Fifth day

Morning: Visit to the **Anne Frank House** (see p. 68).
Afternoon: Lunch and afternoon exploring **the Jordaan** (see p. 77).
Evening: Spend a relaxing evening in a local *proeflokaal* (see p. 122).

▬ *POST OFFICE*

Letters to Europe and postcards for all countries are automatically sent airmail without any surtax. *Lucht postbladen,* or aerograms for overseas destinations, can be purchased at any post office. Stamps are available from the post office, certain news-stands and from automatic distributing machines. The red mailboxes marked PTT are located throughout the city, but make sure you mail your letter in the correct slot: *overige,* for overseas mail. The central post office does not handle packages – go to the sorting office near Centraal Station for these.

Useful addresses

Central post office, Nieuwezidjs Voorburgwal 182, I. B4. ☎ 555 8911; *open Mon-Fri 8:30am-6pm, Thurs to 8:30pm, Sat 9am-noon.*
Sorting office, Oosterdokskade 101, I. A5. *open Mon-Fri 8:30-9pm, Sat 9am-noon.*

▬ *SAFETY PRECAUTIONS*

Amsterdam is not a dangerous city and you can walk safely in any neighbourhood. On the other hand, petty crimes are fairly common, in particular pickpocketing. Be especially careful with your belongings in the red-light district and in the vicinity of Centraal Station, on trams, buses and in crowded areas. Valuable items should be left in your hotel safe, never in your car.

▬ *SHOPPING*

See the section, 'Amsterdam Addresses' p. 117.
Amsterdam is a great place for shopping, especially if your tastes run to gin, flowers and bulbs, cigars or antiques. Amsterdam is one of the international centres for the diamond

Nieuwe Speigelstraat, a busy shopping street and centre of the Amsterdam antique trade.

trade, which has flourished here since the 16th century. Many famous diamonds were cut here, for example the *Cullinan,* which was the largest stone ever found and the *Koh-i-noor,* or 'Mountain of Light,' which belonged to the Mogul emperor before being presented to Queen Victoria. Some of the city's diamond cutting and polishing factories offer free guided tours, giving you an opportunity to see how diamonds are cut:

Amsterdam Diamond Center B.V., Rokin 1, I, C4, ☎ 24 5787.
Bab Hendricksen Diamonds, Weteringschans 89, I, E3, ☎ 26 2798.
Coster Diamonds, Paulus Potterstraat 2-4, I, F2, ☎ 76 2222.
Van Moppes Diamonds, Albert Cuypstraat 2-6, I, F4, ☎ 76 1242.

For generations past, the *Makkum* and *Delfts Blauw* (Delft Blue) pottery has been produced in the workshops of the Netherlands. Authentic delftware is expensive because every piece is hand-painted. You can find it at several shops: **Focke & Meltzer,** P.C. Hoofstraat 65-67, I, E2, ☎ 64 2311; **E. Kramer,** Nieuwe Spiegelstraat 64, I, D3, ☎ 23 0832. Mass-produced imitations are available in souvenir shops and hotel boutiques all over the city.

The city's bustling markets rank among its many attractions, and you can spend a pleasant hour or two strolling through them. The Albert Cuyp, I, F4, is one of the largest daily markets in Europe *(Mon-Sat 9am-4:30pm)* and the 'Bloemenmarkt' (flower market), I, D3, on the banks of the Singel displays hundreds of different flowers all the year round *(Mon-Sat 9am-4:30pm)*.

SIGHTSEEING TOURS

The itineraries, particularly 'The Golden Age' (see p. 67) and 'North-west Amsterdam: The Jordaan' (see p. 77), will take you to the most interesting sites on the canals and in the city. Give yourself two to three hours for these walking tours, unless you wish to spend more time in the museums along the route.

A number of travel agencies organize bus tours of the city, the canals and outlying areas. Since only short distances are involved, you can reach almost all the interesting sites in the Netherlands in one or even half a day. Most of the agencies are located on the Damrak or the Dam; complete information and reservations are available at the VVV offices (see p. 35). For a list of companies operating canal tours, see p. 27. A selective list of other tour operators is given below.

American Express, Damrak 66, I, A4, ☎ 26 2042.

Holland International, Damrak 7, I, A4, ☎ 22 2550.

Keytours, Dam 19, I, B4, ☎ 24 7304.

Lindbergh, Damrak 26, I, A4, ☎ 22 2766.

SPORTS

Bicycling

The Netherlands is an ideal place for cyclists. Bicycles are a common way of getting around the cities and countryside and bicycle lanes are clearly marked. The VVV provides a list of more than 60 bicycle excursions throughout the country. See p. 26 for information concerning bicycle rentals.

Fishing

You can fish all year round in the open sea, but in the inland waters, fishing is allowed June 1 through March 16. A fishing license is required for river, lake, canal and pond fishing; these can be obtained at police stations in the larger cities. For more information, apply to the **NNVS** (Dutch Fishing Association), Postbus 228, 3800 AG Amersfoort, ☎ (033) 63 4924.

Fitness centres

Because of the climate, fitness centres, where you can exercise all year long, are popular. Two of these centres are:

● **Garden Gym,** Jodenbreestraat 158, I, D6, ☎ 26 8772; *open Mon, Wed, Fri 10am-10pm, Thurs 1-10pm, Sun noon-6pm; f9.50 for day ticket.* Here you will find all the facilities you could want, including dance classes, weight training and a sauna.

● **Splash Fitness Club,** Looiersgracht 26-30, I, C2, ☎ 24 8404; *open Mon-Fri 9am-10pm, Sat and Sun 11am-6pm.* Located in the Sonesta Hotel with sauna, aerobics and Turkish bath.

Ice skating

Skating is a national pastime for the Dutch. There are several rinks in Amsterdam, but they can't compare with an exhilarating excursion on its canals or ponds. Be careful on the ice; it is best to follow the example of the Amsterdammers and skate only where you see others skating. For more information, contact the Sport Information Service, ☎ 85 0851.

● **Jaap Eden Baan,** Radioweg 64, ☎ 94 9894; *open Oct-Mar.* This is a large indoor rink, with skate rental possible.

● **Leidseplein rink,** Leidseplein, I, D2; *Open when cold enough.* This is a small free rink.

Swimming pools

● **Mirandabad,** Mirandalaan 9, II, F5, ☎ 44 6637. For water sports, this is the place to go. It is equipped with wave machines, slides, whirlpools and both indoor and outdoor pools.

● **Marnixbad,** Marnixplein 9, I, A2, ☎ 25 4843. Conveniently located in the Jordaan area, this is a covered pool.

● **Zuiderbad,** Hobbemastraat, I, F3, ☎ 79 2217. This covered pool is located near the museums.

▬ TELEPHONE

There are plenty of public telephone booths (painted green) which have instructions printed in several languages. You will need 25 or 100 cent coins. Calls can also be made from restaurants, department stores and most major hotels. The central post office, Nieuwezijds Voorburgwal 182, I, B4, is available for international telephone calls and telegrams 24 hours a day, seven days a week (use the rear entrance on Spuistraat).

International dialing codes
Australia: 09 61.
Canada: 09 1
Great Britain: 09 44.
Ireland: 09 353.
United States: 09 1.

Useful telephone numbers
Directory inquiries: 008.
International directory inquiries: 0018.
Operator: 0010.
Telegrams: 009.

▬ TIME

Like most Western European countries, the Netherlands is one hour ahead of Greenwich Mean Time, six hours ahead of New York and nine hours ahead of Los Angeles.

▬ TIPPING

Service is generally included in restaurant and café checks, which should indicate *inclusief btw* (VAT included). In restaurants where the service has been particularly good, however, it is customary to add 10%. In cafés, round out the figure by adding one or two guilders.

▬ *TOURIST INFORMATION*

The main Amsterdam Tourist Bureau, or VVV, is located at Centraal Stationsplein 10, I. A5, ☎ 22 1016 *(open Easter-Aug, daily 9am-10pm, Sept-Easter, Mon-Sat 9am-5pm, Sun 10am-1pm, 2-5:30pm).* Another VVV office is located at Leidsestraat 106 (same opening hours as Centraal Station VVV office).

You can call for further information, ☎ 26 6444 *(open Mon-Sat 9am-5pm).*

AMSTERDAM IN THE PAST

L ong ago the area where Amsterdam is now located was marshland. The Romans came here (the ruins of one of their forts can be seen at nearby Katwijk) but found nothing attractive in the surroundings. The first-century Roman savant Pliny the Elder wrote of its inhabitants living 'like sailors on a ship, when the surrounding land is flooded.'

The Frisians, as they were known, fished in the Amstel River and in the IJsselmeer Sea. They built mounds of earth to protect themselves and their cattle from the flood waters. They were fiercely independent and successfully fought off several attempts by the Frankish kings to gain control of their territory. Non-Christians, the Frisians fought hard against the Christian missionaries.

BEGINNINGS OF A TRADING EMPIRE

The Frisians began trading in the North and the Baltic seas and became experts in dike building. In the 8th century, the region fell into the hands of Charlemagne and became a stopover on the trade route between Cologne and Britain. For several centuries, control of the region alternated between the German and French kingdoms.

In 1015 a Frisian count succeeded in repelling a German attack and declared himself count of Holland. Power throughout this period and for centuries to come alternated between various counts of Holland, Catholic bishops of Utrecht and counts of Flanders. Political fortunes were subject to the vicissitudes of the lives of royal families, their sons and daughters, and complicated marriage arrangements.

Still nominally under the sovereignty of the bishops of Utrecht, the real local authority remained in the hands of the nobility. A town began growing around the count of Holland's home near the IJ estuary in the 13th century.

The harmonious façade of a former warehouse on Prinseneiland.

A dam was built, giving the town a sea and a river harbour, and in 1275 the count of Holland granted the inhabitants of Aemstelledamme (the dam of the Amstel) toll exemptions. It was the first official reference to the town that was to become the capital of the Netherlands.

Aemstelledamme's first charter in 1300 allowed the town a certain degree of independence in trading and defense matters in exchange for taxes. From this moment until well into the 19th century Amsterdam sought to maintain its independence, resisting any form of external authority, even from the counts of Holland. Money-making matters remained a priority and disruptions to trade and commerce were avoided when possible. The town attempted to stay out of the numerous wars that raged in Europe.

Throughout the 14th century Amsterdam grew, attracting tradespeople, merchants and sailors. The first canals were constructed and buildings such as the Oude Kerk and the Begijnhof monastery (parts of which are still intact) were erected.

Also in the 14th century, William Beukels found a way to preserve herring by gutting and curing them. This seemingly insignificant discovery launched Amsterdam into the merchant trade and is at the root of the saying 'Amsterdam was built on herring bones.' Ships began sailing to Portugal for salt and to Sweden for wood in exchange for fish, cheese and other local products. This trade was to be the source of Amsterdam's economic strength until the 20th century.

A series of noble marriages brought all of Holland, Belgium and Luxembourg into the hands of the dukes of Burgundy in the 15th century. Amsterdam's burgomasters (mayors with considerable authority) and council members were now answerable to the States-General. Burgundy fell, and, as a result of another royal marriage, Maximilian of Austria became the new ruler. In 1489 he granted Amsterdam the right to use the imperial crown on its coat of arms (see p. 74). This symbolic gesture was nonetheless useful for the town in asserting its position as a major port.

Amsterdam was becoming a wealthy, busy city. There were daily markets at the Dam where fish and other goods were sold and financial transactions conducted. Amsterdammers financed their own shipping expeditions and the shipbuilding industry flourished.

THE REFORMATION

At the beginning of the 16th century, the Reformist ideas of Luther began to catch on in mainly Catholic Amsterdam. The more revolutionary and violent Anabaptist sect was also making inroads. At the same time, the Dutch provinces came under the rule of the Catholic king of Spain. When Philip II succeeded to the Spanish throne, he insisted that the heretics be severely punished. Amsterdam's humanist burgomaster who had been reluctant to repress them was replaced: the Inquisition had arrived. Most Amsterdammers were happy to be rid of the Anabaptists, but the repression of other Protestant sects was less to their liking.

Calvinism was gaining ground under the liberal eye of the *stadtholder* of the province, William of Orange. The doctrine of predestination, the sanctioning of usury and the opposition to the authority of the Catholic Church (Calvin believed that man's contact with God was direct and not through intermediaries) appealed to the rich merchant class.

While Calvinism eventually became the fuel in the fight against Spanish oppression, Amsterdam remained essentially Catholic. Its commerce suffered from the anti-Spanish activities of William of Orange and the Protestants.

From 1567 to 1572, Amsterdam opted tragically to back the Spaniards' unsuccessful attempt to subdue most of the other towns of the Netherlands. The tide had turned against the Catholics in Amsterdam. By the end of the decade the town's council was dominated by pro-Calvinists and pro-Orangists. The church was reformed. Catholics were forced to hold services in clandestine churches.

In 1585 the city of Antwerp fell to the Spanish. Antwerp had been the largest port in Europe, a refuge for non-Catholic minorities and Jews who had been expelled from Spain in the 15th century. Amsterdam benefited greatly from the influx of refugees fleeing Catholic oppression: the diamond trade was established, and merchants brought with them capital and the latest in international commercial techniques. It was the beginning of Amsterdam's Golden Age.

THE GOLDEN AGE

During the 17th century Amsterdam became the financial, commercial and cultural centre of Europe. The Wars of Succession against the Spanish who held the southern Netherlands continued intermittently, leaving seven independent provinces, the United Provinces, in the north. When Portugal fell under Spanish control in 1580, Amsterdam's ships no longer had access to Far Eastern goods through the Portuguese. The Dutch East India Company was founded in 1602 and the merchant trade developed. A large building went up on the Dam to house Amsterdam's new financial exchange, complete with 123 offices and shops. For the first time, written drafts were used in transactions instead of coins.

By 1620 there were 100,000 people living in the city. Over the next few decades four new canals were constructed and the city grew from 450 to 1800 acres/182 to 729 hectares. Descartes, who lived on the Westermarkt from 1629 to 1649 found it a perfect place to work '... in this great city everybody except me is in business and so absorbed by profit-making that I could spend my entire life here without being noticed by a soul. I go for a walk every day in the Babel of a great thoroughfare as freely and restfully as you stroll in your garden...'

Descartes found in Amsterdam the freedom he needed to elaborate on his ideas. Other writers such as Gebrand Adriaenszoon Bredero and Joost van den Vondel (see p. 61) were also busy creating some of their greatest works; publishing houses were flourishing; Rembrandt (see p. 74) had moved to the Jewish quarter of Amsterdam and was producing paintings that would earn him a reputation as one of the greatest painters of all time; and a few years after Descartes moved to Amsterdam, the philosopher Baruch Spinoza (see p. 41) was born in a house not far from Rembrandt's. Later he would be influenced by the writings of Descartes (see p. 66).

AMSTERDAM STRIVES TO REMAIN INDEPENDENT

Amsterdam continued to guard its independence fiercely, especially in commercial matters. Much to the dissatisfaction of the United Provinces, the town secretly traded with the Spanish, claiming that the profits enabled it to finance the war. Only when threatened by the Spanish armies would Amsterdam surrender part of its sovereignty to a central authority responsible for defense. As soon as hostilities ceased with the signing of the Treaty of Munster in 1648, separatist trends reemerged.

Acting as a sovereign power, Amsterdam sent its own envoys to negotiate abroad and refused to pay taxes to William II, the Prince of Orange (who represented the States-General, the governing body of the United Provinces). The prince besieged the city in 1650 and, ever intent on avoiding costly fights, Amsterdam surrendered.

In 1672 France and England joined forces to attack the Dutch. The provinces once again united behind the new Prince William of Orange. Louis XIV's advance was checked when the city's dikes were opened, flooding the region. The Prince made a separate peace with England and turned his attention to defeating Louis XIV. Yet, as soon as the fighting ceased, Amsterdam returned to its

Gaily decorated sailboats recall Amsterdam's former trading empire.

anti-Orange stance, conducting its own negotiations with the French.

When Louis XIV invaded Flanders and Luxembourg in 1682, Amsterdam refused to supply the Prince of Orange with troops, thus forcing him to sign a peace treaty. Once again Amsterdam avoided a war and once again the city benefited as the Huguenots fled Louis XIV's persecution of French Protestants. They brought capital and the foundations of a textile industry to Amsterdam.

POLITICAL AND ECONOMIC DECLINE

In 1688 Prince William III of Orange, grandson of England's King Charles I, became King William of

Baruch Spinoza (1632-1677)

Bertrand Russell described Spinoza as the 'noblest and most lovable of the great philosophers,' adding that he was 'ethically supreme.' His father and grandfather were Portuguese Marranos (baptized Jews practicing Judaism in secret) who had fled to Amsterdam to escape the Inquisition. Spinoza received a traditional Jewish education. Since he was a brilliant pupil, his teachers expected him to pursue a scholarly career and to become a rabbi.

He studied Latin and was influenced by Renaissance thinking, especially by Descartes. His doubts and questioning, however, brought him into conflict with the Jewish community, which excommunicated him in 1656. Spinoza changed his name to Benedictus (the Latin equivalent of Baruch) and led a simple life first in Amsterdam and then in The Hague, polishing lenses to eke out a meagre living. His theories, especially his rejection of free will, alienated him from Christians as well.

His greatest work, *Ethics*, was published posthumously. In it he draws ethical conclusions from a rational analysis of God, Nature and Will. According to Spinoza, God and Nature are one. All finite beings and things are aspects of God, and God is in all things. Free will does not exist: all that happens is a manifestation of God's inscrutable nature. He held that human beings could achieve a rational and intellectual knowledge of God's essence and that this knowledge is the 'mind's highest good'.

'We are a part of universal nature and we follow her order,' he wrote.'If we have a clear and distinct understanding of this, that part of our nature which is defined by intelligence... will assuredly acquiesce in what befalls us.' Only through understanding is man free in the sense of being part of the whole and truly achieving a complete intellectual love of God.

Spinoza lived according to his ideas: he was a man of simple needs, generous and perfectly honest. He was a firm advocate of freedom of expression and perhaps for this reason loved Amsterdam, which he described as 'a city like no other, where men of every nation and every religion live together in perfect harmony.' He died of phthisis (a consumptive condition) at the age of 45, serene and free for, as he wrote, 'A free man thinks of nothing less than of death.'

England. The now-powerful king was able to subdue the troublesome Amsterdammer's striving for independence and to concentrate on war against France. Military expenses drained much of Amsterdam's riches, provoking the beginning of the city's decline that was to continue throughout the next century.

Amsterdam's merchant fleet was still one of the largest in the world, with a monopoly on the Baltic trade. The West India Company had lost Brazil and the colonies on the Guyana coast but profits were still available from the sugar trade and the sale of African slaves to South America. The rich merchants of Amsterdam were getting richer even as economic growth was slowing down.

England and France ended their 20-year war in 1712 unified and reinforced. The States of Holland, on the other hand, had lost much of their political power and were soon to lose their financial control. Amsterdam's determination to stay out of big power conflicts and carry on with business was continually thwarted. Unwillingly, the States of Holland were drawn into the War of Austrian Succession and again into war against France.

The Dutch East India Company

Throughout the 16th century, trade in the Indies was dominated by the Portuguese, with the Dutch conducting indirect trade with the Orient through Lisbon. When the Spanish king, Philip II, became monarch of Portugal, these activities were threatened. Amsterdam merchants began exploring the idea of financing their own expeditions to the Indies.

In 1595 nine Amsterdam merchants formed the van Ferne Company and sent Cornelius Houtman with four ships on the first Dutch voyage to the East Indies. He returned two years later, laden with merchandise. Though the expedition itself was not profitable, the Dutch were convinced that direct trade was possible.

In the following years, numerous companies were established to finance trading expeditions to the Orient. The intense competition between the rival groups soon interfered with profitable trade. In 1602 the States-General conducted negotiations between the various companies, which resulted in their merger into the East India Company.

The charter granted by the States-General gave the company monopoly on trade between the Cape of Good Hope and the Straits of Magellan as well as the right to establish strongholds, make treaties and wage wars.

Eight of the 17 constituent members of the company's Chamber were from Amsterdam and the city's merchants subscribed more than half the original capital. Fabulous wealth flowed to Amsterdam as a result: between 1605 and 1642, the dividends paid to shareholders rose from 17 to 50%.

At first the East India Company concentrated on commercial activities, but gradually the Dutch took over the whole of the Indonesian islands, establishing a colonial empire. By the end of the 17th century, the Dutch trading area included India, Ceylon, Malacca and the Malay Archipelago, exceeding the Portuguese empire at its height.

By the end of the century, the growing French and British naval power ended the Dutch monopoly in many regions. Profits began to decline and maintaining order in the colonial territories became too costly. The East India Company governor-general in the mid-18th century complained that 'we are short of everything-good ships, men and officers.'

In 1799 the East India Company was officially liquidated. The colonial empire, though, which it had founded continued in Indonesia until the middle of the 20th century.

By the mid-18th century sugar refineries, sawmills and dye factories were closing down. The merchant trade was still active as was the financial market but industries such as shipbuilding, pottery, brewing, textile and others were declining. Poverty and unemployment were on the rise.

Liberal ideas were taking hold everywhere in Holland and especially among the rising middle class of Amsterdam. Dutch-style liberalism valued commerce and property rights and opposed the hereditary principle, especially as it was used by kings and nobles. A new anti-aristocratic party, the Patriots, gained massive popular support in the city.

Prussia invaded the States of Holland in 1787 and Amsterdam again avoided a potentially bloody fight by surrendering. Four years later the East and West India companies went bankrupt. For the first time since its establishment, the great Exchange Bank of the city could not meet payment demands.

HOLLAND FALLS UNDER FRENCH DOMINATION

In 1795 the French took over the United Provinces. The Patriots, who had gone underground during the Prussian rule, resurfaced in support of the French forces who were welcomed as liberators. Liberty, equality and fraternity were the key words of the period. Yet the atmosphere of jubilation soon died out. The French demanded money to pay the troops, while the English blockaded the coast. When Napoleon took over in France, he set up a separate kingdom of the Netherlands, with Amsterdam as its capital and his brother Louis Napoleon as sovereign.

King Louis' reign was mild but short-lived. He was not as severe as his brother would have liked, especially concerning the clandestine trading between Amsterdam and England. Contraband from England was now systematically burned when discovered. Amsterdammers were outraged both by the loss of profits and what they considered to be an unpardonable waste. Napoleon annexed Holland in 1810 and declared Amsterdam the third city of the French Empire after Paris and Rome.

As the French Empire's troops began suffering defeat at the hands of the advancing Russian and Prussian forces in 1812, the citizens of Amsterdam took to the streets in demonstrations against the emperor.

Traditionally anti-Orangist, Amsterdam hesitated at first to make what was now a necessary move in support of the Prince of Orange. The die, however, was cast. With the arrival of the Cossacks, who mercilessly pillaged and raped, the city realized that it had no other alternative,

---

Multatuli

Eduard Douwes Dekker (1820-1887) went to Asia as a young man to work for the East India Company. In his post as colonial administrator in Java, he was confronted with some of the more brutal aspects of colonialism. He was especially shocked at the abusive treatment of the natives by their Javanese prince, whom the Dutch authorities complaisantly maintained in power.

Dekker quit the company and upon returning to Europe wrote a scathing, if witty, denunciation of colonialism. *Max Havelaar of De Koffie-veilingen van de Nederlandsche Handelsmaatschaapij* (Max Havelaar or The Coffee Auctions of the Dutch Trading Company) was published in Brussels in 1860 under the pseudonym Multatuli (meaning 'I have greatly suffered').

In it the author contrasts the character of the romantic hero Max Havelaar (a sort of self-portrait) with the bourgeois mentality of the coffee broker Batavus Droogstoppel. Multatuli hoped, through his novel, to provoke a drastic change in colonial policy but unlike *Uncle Tom's Cabin,* to which the Dutch often compare it, *Max Havelaar* did not have the intended result.

Nevertheless, it was a literary success and had an enormous influence on Dutch writers of the 19th century. It remains one of the great classics of Dutch literature.

and rallied wholeheartedly behind the Prince of Orange. He was declared sovereign of the Netherlands (including Belgium which was later separated) as King William I on March 30, 1814.

INDUSTRIALIZATION AND RECOVERY

By this time, London had become the financial centre of Europe, and both Rotterdam and Antwerp were drawing away many of Amsterdam's port activities. Amsterdam had permanently lost the central role it occupied during its Golden Age. Yet the city remained one of the commercial centres of Europe and recovery was underway.

A railway was built from the city to Haarlem and another to Utrecht. A public stagecoach system was set up, gas lighting installed and a much-needed sewage disposal service established. A canal from the North Sea to the docks of Amsterdam (built between 1865 and 1876) gave a new impetus to trade. The diamond industry and the money market were revived.

Throughout the latter part of the 19th century and the beginning of the 20th, Amsterdam was busy building and modernizing. The new neo-Gothic Rijksmuseum went up, as did the Stadsschouwburg theatre and the Concertgebouw (whose orchestra became internationally renowned). Trams, horse-drawn at first, made their appearance as did bicycles, which quickly became, and have remained, a popular mode of transportation.

WORLD WAR II: OCCUPATION AND RESISTANCE

On the eve of World War II, Amsterdam had a population of 600,000. Holland remained neutral during the war, but the city nevertheless suffered economically both during the war and in the international depression that followed. In the 1930s unemployment had risen and the small Dutch Nazi party began holding noisy demonstrations. The Amsterdammers responded with massive counter-demonstrations and welcomed thousands of German-Jewish refugees escaping from Nazi Germany.

The Nazis invaded Holland in 1940. While Rotterdam suffered from the five days of Dutch fighting against the German troops, Amsterdam was captured intact. There were approximately 86,000 Jews in the city at the time. The first round-up for deportation on a massive scale took place in February 1941. Amsterdammers were shocked by the brutal treatment of the 400 Jews who were herded onto the Jonas Daniel Meijerplein in the Jewish quarter. Two days later Amsterdam went on a general strike: practically all activity ceased for three days. This was the beginning of the Dutch resistance. Groups formed to manufacture false papers and food coupons and to help Jews and political opponents go into hiding. Three underground newspapers appeared and the resistance movement struck at Nazi targets. Liberation came on May 8, 1945.

In the years following the war, Amsterdam's economy shifted away from the merchant trade, which had thrived on the now-declining East Indian empire. The diamond industry was reestablished, despite the death in the concentration camps of approximately 70,000 of the city's Jews, many of whom were in the diamond trade. A new fashion industry developed, and Amsterdam became one of the tourist capitals of Europe. International companies, such as IBM, set up their European headquarters here.

Chronology of historical events

1275	'Aemstelledamme' is first mentioned as a small village of fishermen and traders in a charter issued by Floris IV, count of Holland.
1300	The town acquires administrative and legal autonomy.
1452	A great fire destroys almost all the wooden houses; henceforth, houses are built in brick.
1473	The entire country is governed by the powerful House of Burgundy.
1515	Charles I of Spain inherits the Netherlands. In 1519 he becomes emperor of Germany under the name of Charles V.
1520	Charles V seeks to stop the spread of Protestantism and the Inquisition is established.
1572	William of Nassau, Prince of Orange, heads the uprising of the Provinces against Spain: this is the beginning of the 80-year war.
1581	The seven Protestant provinces, including Amsterdam (known as the Republic of the United Provinces), achieves independence from Spain. This marks the beginning of Amsterdam's 'population explosion' (the number of inhabitants rises from 30,000 to 200,000).
1600	Beginning of the Golden Age, thanks to the philosophers (Erasmus), the artists (Rembrandt) and the merchants and explorers (Houtman). Creation of the East India Company, followed by a commercial expansion and the foundation of a great colonial empire. Amsterdam becomes the main port and the largest market in the world.
1648	Treaty of Munster: end of the war with Spain.
1652-1667	Series of wars with England.
1700-1800	Stagnation of the country's national development.

COUNTER-CULTURE AND LIBERALISM

The municipal council, dominated by Socialists, instituted liberal policies in many domains. In the mid-60s what had started as a literary-philosophical group known as the Provos (for provocation) became a radical political movement. The Provos were against middle-class values, big business and pollution (they supplied free bicycles around town in an attempt to replace cars). Many of their demonstrations ended in street battles (using cobblestones as weapons) against the police.

Amsterdam became the centre of the counter-culture, the hippie capital of the world. Youth flocked here to take advantage of the liberal atmosphere. John Lennon and Yoko Ono staged their eight-day bed-in at

1780	The Anglo-Dutch conflict marks the beginning of British naval supremacy, contributing to the decline of Amsterdam's prosperity.
1795	Napoleon's armies invade the United Provinces; French domination lasts 20 years.
1815	Following the battle of Waterloo William of Orange is recognized as king of the Netherlands. The establishment of the monarchy, which still endures, marks the birth of the modern Netherlands.
1865	For the first time since the Golden Age, economic growth once again leads to a considerable increase in Amsterdam's population. By the end of the 19th century, Amsterdam has recovered its economic and cultural vigour.
1890	Reign of Queen Wilhelmina.
1920	Beginning of land reclamation projects.
1940-1945	Second World War. A terrible tragedy for Amsterdam's inhabitants, 10% of whom die, primarily those of Jewish descent.
1948	Abdication of Queen Wilhelmina in favour of her daughter Juliana.
1949	Independence of Dutch Indies.
1954	Autonomy granted to Dutch Guyana (Suriname).
1957	Admission of the Netherlands to the EEC. Beginning of Amsterdam's renewed cultural influence.
1960	Benelux economic union comes into force.
1975	Independence of the Republic of Suriname.
1980	Queen Juliana abdicates in favour of her daughter Beatrix.

Amsterdam's Hilton Hotel in 1969. There was an influx of drugs into the city.

The worried municipality responded with liberal policies concerning soft drugs: the possession of marijuana in small quantities was de-criminalized, and places were set up where people could smoke marijuana – unofficially but unhindered. Simultaneously the police clamped down on hard drugs.

While these events were making international headlines, the majority of Amsterdammers were living their quiet, traditional lives. Often appalled and disgusted by the hippies, whom they considered to be dirty, they remained tolerant, in true Amsterdam style. On several occasions when the municipal government was planning to demolish historical sectors of town, the Provos were able to muster the support of much of the city's population.

Amsterdammers realized that their city was special. Its historical heritage, its canals, small cafés, cobblestoned streets and squares needed to be preserved in order to preserve the quality of life – unstressed and leisurely – that Amsterdam cherishes.

AMSTERDAM TODAY

Amsterdam is the capital of the Netherlands although it is neither the seat of government (located in The Hague) nor the residence of the queen, who lives at Soestdijk. Moreover, it has lost its historical position as the country's major port to Rotterdam. Nevertheless, Amsterdam is the economic and cultural centre of the country. Amsterdammers consider their city the heart of the Netherlands.

It is located at the mouth and on the south bank of the IJ, the inland arm of the IJsselmeer. Divided into two parts by the Amstel River, the whole city has been built on land reclaimed from the sea. Almost all of it is located at about 12 ft/3.7 m below sea level.

Amsterdam is protected by a series of jetties and dikes; the canals were designed to drain off water and to dry out land. Buildings are constructed on piles driven 40 to 66 ft/12 to 20 m into the varying layers of sand. There are millions of piles in the city, though the exact number is unknown. The Royal Palace at the Dam, for example, rests on 13,600 piles and Centraal Station on 26,000. To ensure stability, many of the very old buildings need to have their foundations renewed, a costly procedure that weighs on the city's budget.

ECONOMY

Amsterdam is Holland's major industrial, manufacturing and financial centre. Of the half a million employees in the Greater Amsterdam area, 23% work in manufacturing. The key manufacturing industries based in the capital include metallurgy, chemicals, food and beverages (for example, Heineken) and transportation equipment (Fokker Aircraft).

The sectors of wholesale and retail trade employ 20% of the population; another 17% is active in finance and business-related services. Most of the Dutch banks and insurance companies have their headquarters here, and the foreign securities exchange is one of the most active in Europe.

The municipal government employs 12% of the working population, while health and social services account for 13%, transportation for 10%, hotels and restaurants for 3% and agriculture for 2%.

Approximately 2.2 million foreign tourists visit Holland annually bringing in revenues of 850 million guilders. An additional 900 million guilders a year is spent in Amsterdam by Dutch visitors. The nearby Schiphol International Airport is another important source of income. The airport serves 14.5 million passengers and transports 758,000 tons (758 million kilos) of freight each year.

Despite the relative health of many individual economic sectors, unemployment in the capital is extremely high (24.3% in 1987). The city budget experienced a record deficit of 12 million guilders in 1988. The following year, the municipality made important budgetary cuts, especially in the domain of cultural and social services, with the goal of drastically reducing the deficit. Most of the municipal budget is devoted to maintenance of the city's infrastructure (transportation, electricity, etc.) and the construction and renovation of roads, bridges and buildings.

PRESERVATION OR URBAN RENEWAL?

The desire of Amsterdammers to preserve their magnificent historical heritage while meeting the requirements of a modern city is a major challenge. One of the biggest problems facing Amsterdam over the past two decades has been housing. Residential space in the city centre is limited and it is difficult to increase living space without demolishing historical buildings or causing an exodus of commerce to the outskirts.

Since the early 1970s, the urban area has doubled and many former inner-city dwellers have moved to the suburbs. Owners of property in the centre often opted to leave their houses empty and sell them later at a higher price since rent control policies and the difficulty in evicting inhabitants made renting property unattractive.

This infuriated leftist youth groups in the 70s and contributed to the rise of a militant squatter movement. Empty buildings were occupied; the police would periodically move in to evict the illegal inhabitants, often resulting in street fights between the squatters, armed with cobblestones, and the police.

The movement mustered a good deal of popular support in its opposition to the destruction of working-class districts. Despite widespread protests, both the Nieuwmarkt and Waterlooplein neighbourhoods were profoundly changed during construction of the subway in the 70s.

Over the past few years, the squatter movement has declined. New and more restrictive property laws were instituted and the police learned how to deal with evictions while avoiding violence. In an attempt to preserve the city centre's residential and commercial character, a new urban plan was drawn up by the municipal government in 1985. The plan clearly outlines the city's intention to preserve a compact centre. Buildings are being renovated wherever possible. In areas such as the Nieuwmarkt and Waterlooplein, architects Téo Bosch, Rudy Uytenhaak and Paul de Ley have designed modern housing that is rooted in the traditions of Amsterdam.

Traffic congestion and the resulting pollution are two other major problems in Amsterdam. During the Provos' heyday (see p. 47), ecologists demanded that cars be banished in favour of bicycles. Here and there you will see a few 'witcars,' electrically powered vehicles (the last survivors of the Provos' campaigns) but they are not widely used. However, bicycles remain one of the preferred modes of transportation: about 20% of the population uses one to get to work.

To further alleviate traffic on the narrow streets and bridges of the city centre, parking lots have been placed around the periphery, and service on the public trams, buses and the rapid transit system (opened in 1977) is continually improved.

A highway that encircles the city is under construction, which will facilitate access.

There are no ghettos in Amsterdam but the poor tend to live in the south-east and west sections of the city. The more wealthy reside mainly along the canals and in the south around the Vondelpark.

TOLERANCE: A TRADITIONAL DUTCH IDEAL

Foreigners, known as *outlanders,* make up almost 23% of the city's population. There are also large communities originating from the former Dutch colonies of Indonesia and Suriname. Amsterdammers, though known for their traditional tolerance of foreigners and minorities, have experienced difficulties integrating some of these groups – in particular the large, and poor,

Holland is world renowned for its production of Gouda and Edam cheese.

Surinamese population, the Moroccans and the Turks.

Yet, despite inevitable conflicts stemming from disparate ways of life and economic conditions, Amsterdam has remained true to its tradition. In 1983, when a young black man was knifed during a brawl, Amsterdammers were deeply shocked. A memorial was erected in the Vondelpark with the inscription. 'May Amsterdam remain a centre of tolerance.'

Resident foreigners have had the right to vote in municipal elections since 1986 (when 20 *outlanders* were elected as representatives in the country). There are 25 mosques today in Amsterdam. Several television programs are specifically oriented toward foreigners: 'Passport,' for example, broadcasts programs in Turkish, Arabic, Spanish, Italian and Serbo-Croatian.

Amsterdam's police force has embarked upon a program of minority recruitment with the stated goal of having 25% women and 10% former immigrants (naturalization procedures are accelerated for candidates) by the beginning of the 1990s.

These policies are typical of the liberal ideas of Amsterdam's city council, which has been dominated by the Socialists since the end of World War II. The council consists of 45 members who are elected for a four-year term; an executive committee of nine elected aldermen; and the burgomaster (mayor), who is appointed by the queen for a six-year term. The municipal administration handles all public services and many social and welfare services; it has its own banks and printing shop and owns many of the city's public buildings and recreation areas.

Some of the city's liberal policies, concerning in particular soft drugs, prostitution and pornography, have contributed to Amsterdam's reputation as a permissive town. Amsterdam's prostitutes in the brothels (as opposed to those who work on the streets) pay taxes and benefit from free medical checkups; many accept travelers checks.

Located in the historical heart of the city, the red-light district surprises visitors by its cleanliness and propriety compared to any other district of its kind in Europe or North America.

Possession of marijuana or hash is considered a misdemeanor. There are dozens of cafés where these soft drugs can be purchased openly and even found listed, complete with prices, on menus. On the other hand, the police work hard to stem the traffic of hard drugs. In fact, despite its reputation as a drug haven, Amsterdam has no more drug addicts than any other of Europe's major capitals. Furthermore, the city's drug addicts can seek help in overcoming their addiction in numerous drug centres.

AMSTERDAM AND ART

Amsterdam's cultural life is extremely active. The orchestra of the Concertgebouw, conducted by Bernard Haitink, is world renowned, as are some of its ballet and modern dance companies.

Many of Amsterdam's painters are internationally famous. Their work is often exhibited in the city's modern museums and in many of its more than 200 galleries.

Among the more prominent contemporary painters is abstract expressionist Jan Siehuis, who creates a highly personal style with brilliant colours and intense paint strokes. Ger Lataster's paintings evoke abstract if identifiable images through stark contrasting colours.

Other contemporary painters include Ger Van Elk, Kees Smits and Marien Schouten. Two of Amsterdam's most outstanding sculptors are Leo Voegindeweij who creates enthralling forms out of lead and aluminium cement; and Richard Meitner, who is internationally renowned for his glass art.

Video artists include Christiaan Bastiaans and Kees de Groot. The latter combines video, music, performance and painting. Other multi-media performances have been created by Jaap de Jonge and the group Sluik/Kurpershoes.

The two most celebrated Dutch film-makers are Paul Verhoeven and Fons Rademakers. Rademakers won an Oscar in 1987 for his film based on the book by Dutch writer Harry Mulisch, *The Assault*.

Mulisch is Amsterdam's best-known contemporary novelist. His mother was a Belgian Jew who escaped to the United States during the occupation, his father an Austrian banker who collaborated with the Nazis and was imprisoned after the war. The Nazi occupation and its repercussions for people living in modern-day Amsterdam is the subject of *The Assault*. His recent novels *Last Call* and *The Assault* have both been translated into English.

Other post-war novelists who have been inspired by the war are Gerard Reve *(The Evenings)* and W.F. Hermans *(The Dark Room of Damocles)*. Several other writers have had their books translated abroad: Cees Nooteboom's *Rituals* (1978) received the Pegasus Mobil Prize, and Martin 't Hart (one of Holland's most widely read authors) earned considerable international respect when his 1979 *Bearers of Bad Tidings* was translated into English.

Until recently Amsterdam's art scene thrived on substantial government subsidies. Artists were given a basic revenue that covered living and working costs. Budgetary constraints, though, have forced the government to diminish subsidies. While established artists remain generally unaffected by these changes, many of the city's numerous young artists are worried about their future.

I
THE HISTORIC
HEART OF THE CITY

A msterdam grew on the site of a small fishing port and the Amstel lies at its centre. The canals dug to drain off water from the swampy ground have become an extensive network of urban communication. The city's original limits were marked by the Singel but a semi-circle of new canals was built which curved toward the firm ground.

Around the Dam – the heart of the medieval city and the site of the first dike – many street names serve as reminders that this was once a port. Damrak (*rak* meaning port), for example, refers to the outer port, and Rokin, which derives from *Rak-in*, means the inner port. Trading began in the vicinity of the Dam although nothing in the present-day bustle of tourists and shoppers reflects the former activity of these streets. However, you will see some remnants of the fortifications that surrounded the city toward the end of the 15th century: the **Muiderpoort,** the **Sint Antoniespoort,** which later became the **Wag** (the Weights and Measures Keep) and one or two towers such as the **Schreierstoren** (the Weepers' Tower), the **Regulierspoort** (now the Munttoren or Mint) and the **Montelbaanstoren.**

The churches, which unfortunately have been abandoned or extensively restored, include the **Oude Kerk** (Old Church) and the **Nieuwe Kerk** (New Church). Almost everywhere along this route you will see delightful houses with access directly onto the water to facilitate the unloading of goods (in Warmoesstraat, for example, along the Nieuwendijk).

This itinerary takes approximately four hours. Allow several hours more if you want to visit the museums along this route.

▬ *THE DAM* ★★ I, B4

The **Dam** is the best place to start. It is the largest square in the Netherlands and major ceremonies are held here. The site of the dike that was the city's very foundation, the Dam is the heart of the country and Amsterdam's forum.

In the center of the square is the Bevrijdingsmonument, the national liberation monument designed by the sculptor Rae-decker to commemorate the Dutch men and women who died during World War II. Concerts and art exhibits are organized in the square throughout the year. Two buildings dominate the square: the **Royal Palace** and the **New Church** (Nieuwe Kerk).

The Royal Palace ** (Koninklijk Paleis) I, B4

One-hour guided tours are given daily July-Aug., 12:30-4pm; f1 admission charge.

Guided tours may also be arranged during the rest of the year. For information, apply to the Educational Service of the Palace, ☎ (020) 24 8698.

The queen is in residence only occasionally. She usually lives at Soestdijk and carries out her official duties in The Hague.

With the growth of the city in the 17th century, Jacob van Campen, the most famous Dutch architect of his day, was invited to design a new town hall. The building, constructed on 13,659 wooden piles, is considered particularly charac-teristic of the Dutch classical style, and its imposing proportions symbolize to perfection a city at the height of its expansion. The decoration of the interior was done by some of the most celebrated artists of the time, with the exception of Rembrandt, whose work was rejected.

Construction of the town hall began on January 2, 1648, and the first section was inaugurated by the burgomaster and his deputies on July 29, 1655. The work wasn't completed, however, until the next decade.

Damaged by fire, the building was restored by Louis Bona-parte and converted into a royal residence in 1808. When Bonaparte abdicated in 1810, he left behind a superb collec-tion of Empire furniture. The state purchased the hall from the city of Amsterdam in 1930.

The New Church ** (Nieuwe Kerk) I, B4

Open Mon-Sat 11am-4pm, Sun noon-3pm; closed Jan and Feb.

A flamboyant Gothic building inspired by the French style and dating from 1408, the church burned down on several occasions. It was rebuilt and underwent alterations several times, most recently in the 17th century by Jacob van Campen, the architect of the Royal Palace. The spire remains unfinished. The history of the New Church is intimately linked with the history of the Dutch Royal House. Ever since the birth of the Kingdom of the Netherlands, all the corona-tions have taken place here.

The Nieuwe Kerk is famous for its marvelous stained-glass windows, the most noteworthy is in the north transept on the Nieuwe Zijds Voorburgwal. This is the oldest window and is the work of Johannes Gerritsz Bronkhorst (1650).

It depicts Count William IV who in 1342 bestowed his coat of arms on the city. The large window overlooking the south transept was a gift from the Dutch people on the occasion of Queen Wilhelmina's coronation. It depicts all the princes of Orange since William the Silent.

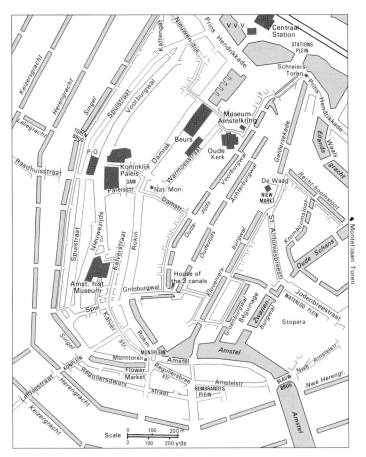

Itinerary I

Of particular interest are the copper choir screen, by Lutma, and the magnificent *Chair of Truth* with carvings representing Divine Mercy, the cardinal virtues and the Evangelists. The hexagonal form of the chair rests on six angels, and the corners are embellished with six statues representing Perseverance, Hope, Love, Faith, Justice and Truth. Between these figures stand the four Evangelists with their symbols. The pillar supporting the chair is made up of wooden panels: the centre panel depicts the Last Judgment, the right-hand panel the parable of the Foolish Virgins and the Wise Virgins, and the left-hand panel the parable of the Talents.

The remarkable funeral monuments are an essential feature of the Nieuwe Kerk's interior. A number of famous figures from the history of the Netherlands are buried here, notably sailors of the Golden Age, including Admiral Michiel Adriaansz de Ruyter and Commander Jan van Galen whose tomb was designed by Quellijn. The sea battle is the work of sculptor Willem de Keyser and the recumbent statue is by Rombout Verhulst.

The church also contains the tomb of Admiral J.H. van Kinsbergen who was buried here in 1819 as well as the modest tomb of J.C. van Speijck, an Amsterdam orphan who became a celebrated naval hero and was killed in 1832. A man who might be called the greatest Amsterdammer of all time, even though he was born in Cologne, is also buried here: poet and writer Joost van den Vondel (see p. 61).

■■■ *FROM THE DAMSTRAAT TO THE NIEUWMARKT* I, B4-5

Leaving the Dam (on the side where the Hotel Krasnapolsky is located), take the **Damstraat,** a busy commercial street where you can find almost any type of restaurant. Turn right when you reach the **Oude Zijds Voorburgwal** ✦✦. Houses ornamented with gables and coats of arms line both sides of this canal. Particularly worth noting are: n° 187, a fine sculpted gable (1663); n° 231, a sumptuous stone doorway of the Illustrious Athenaeum (1632), which now belongs to the university; and n° 298, a very attractive doorway by Brakke Grond (1624). Several houses at n° 300 were converted in 1614 to become the state pawnshop; it is currently the headquarters of the Municipal Savings Bank. Poet Joost van den Vondel was employed here for ten years as an accountant.

At the end of Enge Lombardsteeg alley, turn right on the **Grimburgwal,** which lies in the heart of the university district. There are a number of charming shops and student cafés on this typical small canal. You might also try the pancakes at **Carla Ingeborg's Pannenhuis,** situated on the first floor of n° 2, a lovely 16th-century house.

Turn back along the Grimburgwal (the university is on your right) and cross the bridge. At the intersection of Oude Zijds Voorburgwal and Oude Zijds Achterburgwal, I, C4, you will see the **House of the Three Canals** ✦ (Driegrachtenhuis, 1609) with its red shutters and stained-glass windows. Now a publishing firm, it was built by a noble family on the south-east edge of the medieval town. The embankment used to be known as the *Fluurelenburgwal,* or Velvet Embankment, because the wealthy burgesses who lived there dressed in silk and velvet.

Continue across the bridge and take O.Z. Achterburgwal to the left until you reach the carved doorway at the beginning of the **Oudemanhuispoort,** a narrow street with bookstalls and shops selling old prints. At one time this street led to the Old People's Home *(oude mannen),* which is now the main administrative building of the university.

Leaving the arcade, turn to the right on Kloveniers Burgwal. Cross the first bridge on your left, and continue straight to the Staalstraat until you reach the Groenburgwal; then turn left. There is a splendid view in the direction of the Zuiderkerk. The English Church at n° 42 was the former home of Hendrik De Keyser, mayor of the city from 1565 to 1621. The house at n° 40 is a converted warehouse with an Indonesian name, *Malang,* recalling the colonial era. Take Raamgracht to your left and turn right on Kloveniers Burgwal; you will see some delightful classical gables. The **Trippenhuis,** a large

The Oudekerk, built in 1309, is Amsterdam's oldest church.

Renaissance house at n° 29, is now the seat of the Koninklijke Nederlandse Akademie van Wetenschappen, the Royal Netherlands Academy of Science. It was built in 1660 by the two Trip brothers, who were mine owners and arms manufacturers.

The two brothers tossed a coin to decide how the house should be divided between them. In 1842, after complex negotiations, the last owner, the great-grandson of one of the brothers, persuaded the city to purchase the huge building.

Almost directly opposite at n° 26, stands a house built by a man with more modest ambitions. He was a coachman employed by one of the brothers and was satisfied with a house not much larger than the doorway of his master's home. The result was this tiny but enchanting Baroque dwelling.

Take a look inside the herbal drugstore of **Jacob Hooy and Co. *** at n° 12. For 140 years the same family has sold 500 to 600 varieties of herbs and spices, together with 35 kinds of tea and 38 kinds of *drops* (a typical Dutch licorice that is usually salty).

You have now come to the **Nieuwmarkt** (New Market;l, B5), which in spite of its name is the oldest in the city. In addition to the market itself, there are a number of shops and bars and, on New Year's Eve, groups of artists organize a tremendous fireworks display. An antiques fair is held from May to September (10am-5pm).

The Waag l, B4

In the middle of this large square where a small market manages to survive among all the cars, you will see **St Antony's Gate **** (Sint Antoniespoort), a relic of the 15th-century medieval city. This vast, square edifice flanked by round towers has been known as the Waag since the 17th-century. At that time it ceased to be a bastion on the outskirts of the city and became the Public Office of Weights (*waag* is derived from *wegen,* meaning to weigh). The upper level was made available to various guilds, including the Guild of Surgeons. In 1632, Rembrandt, barely 26 years old, painted the picture here that made him famous, *The Anatomy Lesson of Dr. Tulp* (Mauritshuis, The Hague). Dr. Tulp was the chief surgeon of the guild and commissioned the painting to record a lesson in the physiology of the arm, which he gave in January 1632. The master surgeon is shown surrounded by his students and admirers.

Nieuwmarkt l, B4

Nieuwmarkt is the first station of the subway; its construction sparked violent disturbances in the 1970s. It was impossible to build the subway directly below the surface because of the spongy subsoil. The only solution was to build it above ground and then cover it up, but this meant that certain areas on the proposed line would have to be demolished. The Nieuwmarkt area, an integral part of the old Jewish quarter, was particularly threatened. With the backing of the surviving Provos and other pressure groups, the inhabitants organized protests that sometimes degenerated into riots. The most violent clashes, which took place on March 24, 1975, were nothing short of pitched battles. These events are recorded in an exhibition in the Nieuwmarkt subway station!

▬ *FROM THE MONTELBAAN TOWER TO THE WEEPERS' TOWER* l, AB5-6

Behind the Waag go straight along the right side of Gelders-kade (there is a fine coat of arms at the tobacco shop at n° 8) and then turn on the Rechtbloomsloot which is lined with 17th- and 18th-century houses and warehouses as well as new buildings. When you come to the Oude Schans, once an inland port, turn to the left.

Montelbaan Tower l, B6

Directly in front of you is the head office of the Municipal Water Supply Company. The tower was constructed in 1512

Joost van den Vondel (1587-1679)

Joost van den Vondel was the national poet during Holland's Golden Age and today is considered to be the father of Dutch poetry. His parents were Mennonites who were forced to flee from religious persecution in Antwerp and settled first in Cologne (where Vondel was born) and then in Amsterdam.

In January 1638 the new classical theatre opened with a performance of one of his tragedies, *'Gijsbreght van Aemstel,'* which parallels the liberation of Amsterdam in the Middle Ages after a siege of several weeks, to the liberation announced by the birth of Christ. At the same time, it compares the treachery that led to the fall of Amsterdam to the Massacre of the Innocents in Bethlehem. Similarly, the destruction of Amsterdam by fire is compared to the destruction of Troy as described by Virgil. The play is rhetorical rather than tragic. It has become an Amsterdam tradition, performed every New Year.

Vondel's other poems include a tribute to Jacob van Campen (1655), the architect of the Royal Palace, in which he celebrates the pride, piety and confidence of a people who succeeded in winning their independence and triumphing over Spain, then the dominant power in the world.

The poet was a remarkably prolific writer whose works touched on many of the significant problems of his time. His style, though somewhat ponderous, exhibits a mastery of form and a vehemence that has earned him a place as possibly the greatest poet in Dutch history.

---

to protect the dry dock and the shipyards, but by 1606 it had ceased to be a means of defense. Today it looks out on only a few old barges and house boats.

The VOC Head Office I, B6

When you reach the end of the canal, cross the bridge to the right. Facing the sea on the corner of Prins Hendrikkade, I, B6, is a large red and yellow building dating from 1642. This is the former head office of the **Dutch East India Company** ★ (p. 43), recalling the era when Amsterdam sent its sailors and merchants on all the sea routes of the East Indies in search of spices and other sources of wealth. The building's dimensions give an impression of austerity and grandeur. The warehouse and meeting room bear the initials VOCA (the 'A' indicates that this was the Amsterdam office). The building is a perfect reflection of the famous company, the largest trading organization in the world in the 17th century, which developed into a military and diplomatic power whose sole concerns were profit and efficiency. This is the oldest of the company's many warehouses.

The port opposite serves as a reminder of the site's former shipping activities. But the ships that once unloaded their precious cargoes are no more than a memory. There is, however, one striking symbol of the Orient: the green pagoda roof of the Sea Palace, a floating Chinese restaurant.

Go right and cross the bridge at the corner of Prins Hendrik-kade and Kattenburger Straat.

The Netherlands Maritime Museum ★★ (Nederlands Scheepvaart Museum) II, B5

Open Tues-Sat 10am-5pm, Sun and holidays 1-5pm; f5 admission charge.

This vast museum is housed in the former naval arsenal, built in 1656. There is a gigantic array of historical models, paintings, charts, instruments and weapons, illustrating every aspect of the Netherlands' maritime history: the merchant marine, the navy, the fishing fleets and so on. The inner courtyard contains cannons from 17th-and 18th-century ships. There are also several historic vessels: the 1818 royal launch, for example, with its gold-leaf decoration; a sailing lugger used for herring fishing (1912), moored at the landing stage; a steam icebreaker; and a lifeboat.

East along the Kattenburger Gracht is the area known as *Oosterlijke Eilanden,* the Eastern Isles, which were once the docks of the Admiralty, the VOC shipyards and the scores of private shipyards. Peter the Great worked at the VOC shipyards in 1697-98 to learn shipbuilding techniques.

Retrace your steps along the Prins Hendrikkade. At n° 131, a coat of arms formed by three ships with wooden hulls and spread sails indicates the residence of Michael Adriaanszoon De Ruyter. He was a famous admiral of the Dutch fleet who defeated the Franco-British fleet in 1671 and was killed in the Gulf of Syracuse in 1676 during a battle with a French squadron.

The Weepers' Tower * (Schreierstoren) I, A5

At n° 95 is the Weepers' Tower (1569), a massive semi-circular relic of the rampart that protected Amsterdam in the Middle Ages. It has been converted into a shop selling nautical books and instruments.

The first expedition to the East Indies set out from here in 1595. It ended up in America in a bay later named after the captain, Henry Hudson. Tradition has it that the tower owes its name (*schreien* means to weep) to the many tears shed here by the sailors' wives and sweethearts. Whenever a convoy set sail for the East Indies on a voyage, which sometimes lasted for years, the women would come here to bid their men farewell and to watch the ships until they disappeared over the horizon. The façade bears the image of a ship heading seaward and a weeping woman.

▬▬ *AMSTELKRING, OUDE KERK AND THE RED-LIGHT DISTRICT* I, B5

Behind the tower, take the second canal, Oude Zijdskalk (completely renovated), to the left and then Sint Olofssteeg to Oude Zijds Voorburgwal. You are in the very heart of the 'red-light district,' also known as *Walletjes*. The *Walletjes* is given over to sex shops and prostitutes who wait for clients behind windows surrounded by little red lamps. Prostitutes in Amsterdam have their own union. The district is comparatively quiet at nightfall. There are numerous cafés and small restaurants where you can get very cheap meals.

Amstelkring Museum ** I, B5

Open Mon-Sat 10am-5pm, Sun and holidays 1-5pm: f3 admission charge.

Popularly known as *Ons Lieve Heer op Zolder*, Our Good Lord in the Attic, this is the only clandestine Catholic church remaining from the period after the Reformation when Catholics worshipped in secret *Schuilkerken*. There were 26 *Schuilkerken* in 1881.

The courtyard of the Beguine Convent is an enclave of tranquillity near busy Spui Square.

Dedicated to St Nicholas, the church is hidden beneath the roof of a classical building similar to those around it. In its present state it dates from about 1735 (Catholic ceremonies were conducted there until the end of the 18th century). It contains statues and silverware, a Baroque altar and an 18th-century organ with hand-operated bellows.

You will also see the 17th-century *Sael,* a perfectly preserved sitting room in the classic Dutch style, two kitchens, the priest's bedroom with its genuine alcove and a gallery of paintings including works by the portrait-painter Thomas de Keyser. Several other small rooms, steep stairways and concealed corners, with their splendid furnishings and admirable paintings, embody the feeling of the Golden Age. A few yards away is the more elaborate *Oude Kerk.*

The Old Church * (Oude Kerk) I, B5

Forty-five-minute tours of the tower are given June 1-Sept 15, Mon and Thurs 2-5pm, Tues-Wed 11am-2pm.
Dedicated to St Nicholas until 1578 (in the distance you will see the present St Nicholas Church), the Old Church was built in 1309 in the Gothic style. It was subsequently modified, notably in the 16th century. This accounts for the mixture of Dutch Gothic and Renaissance styles. Below the south porch to the right of the sacristy are the arms of Maximilian of Austria and Philip the Fair who contributed to the financing of the building.

The slender octagonal bell tower (1564), a Gothic construction with certain Renaissance embellishments, the work of Joost Bilhamer, is typical of many Amsterdam buildings. It was once a beacon for sailors.

In 1566, the year the first Protestant sermon was preached, the people destroyed the statues of saints and other 'Papist' figures in the church. If you enter through the door of the sacristy and go around the church from the right, you will see a stained-glass window depicting the coat of arms of the Amsterdam burgomasters from 1578 to 1767 and another displaying the *Netherlands Declaration of Independence*. Nearby are three windows painted by Pieter Aertsz (1508-1575) illustrating the *Immaculate Conception,* the *Visitation* and the *Nativity* together with the *Dormition* (death of the Virgin).

To the left opposite, against one of the choir pillars, is the tomb of Admiral J. van Heemskerk (1567-1607), who tried to discover a passage to the Indies by the Arctic Ocean and was killed off Gibraltar during a battle against the Spaniards. In the aisle to the left is the tomb of Rear Admiral van der Zaan (died 1669). In the right-hand aisle are the tombs of Admiral T. Sweers, killed in a battle won by the combined French and English fleets (August 22, 1637) and Vice-Admiral Abr. van der Hulst (died 1666). Against one of the choir pillars is the tomb of Admiral Cornelis Jan (died 1633). Saskia, Rembrandt's wife, is buried here under a tombstone bearing the inscription K.19, Saskia.

Engerkerkstraat will bring you to Warmoesstraat, one of Amsterdam's oldest streets. Before the 16th century it was a flower market; today there are numerous sex shops, night-clubs and restaurants. Take a look at the superb old decor inside the tea and coffee dealers at n° 66.

The Oudebrugsteeg leads to the impressive brick building that houses the Stock Exchange; its dimensions reflect Amsterdam's financial importance.

The building was designed in 1903 by the architect Petrus Berlage who inspired a school that had a considerable influence on the country's architecture.

Next door is the Stock Market built by Berlage's teacher J.H. Cuijpers.

▬ *AROUND THE DAMRAK* I, AB4

You are now on the Damrak which, with its hotels, restaurants, money changers, souvenir shops and travel agencies, is the city's tourist centre.

Take one of the narrow streets in front of you, which lead to Nieuwendijk, a pedestrian-only shopping street.

Turn immediately to the left when you come to the Singel (there is a stall on the locks near the port where you can sample herrings with or without onions).

Beside n° 7 is the old Lutheran church (built *c.* 1670, restored in the 19th century and now used by the Sonesta Hotel for promenade concerts on Sunday mornings). Here is the narrowest house in Amsterdam, consisting of a single doorway with a window above it. It was built to block an alleyway.

Almost opposite is Poezenboot, a barge converted into a home for cats (visit 1-2pm; donations accepted).

The oldest of Amsterdam's hotels, the Broumer hotel (1652), is located at n° 83.

Cross over to the other bank. The large red brick house at n° 140 was the home of Captain Frans Banning Cocq (1605-1655), who was painted by Rembrandt with his Company of Arquebusiers.

In front of you is the **Torenburg** ★, I, B3, which was a prison tower in the Middle Ages.

Cross the bridge (there is a very fine view of the Westerkerk to the left) and continue along the Singel. Look at the façades of the houses lining this canal that was part of the city's fortification system in the early 17th century. At n° 210 is an old depot ★ (1737) that has been converted into a res- taurant-tearoom, **De Roo Oly Molen.**

Follow the Singel to reach **Spui Square,** I, C3, where you can buy foreign newspapers and magazines at the Atheneum Bookshop. Opposite is the popular Hoppe Café which is often crowded with Amsterdammers meeting for a drink after work. In the middle of the square is the statue of the *Hieuerdje* (Little Darling). Donated to the city by a cigarette company, the statue was a target of Provo attacks during the 1960s (see p. 47).

If you cross Spui Square, you can see a narrow street with no doors in the façades on your left and just opposite a university building. Between n° 37 and n° 38 there is a gateway with a coat of arms depicting a virgin protecting several women and bearing the inscription *Begijnhof.* This leads to a large courtyard in which there is a church flanked by small houses.

The Beguine Convent (Begijnhof) I, C3

The Beguines were a lay order of nuns, established here in 1369. After two years' novitiate and six years in a convent, they made a non-perpetual vow of obedience and retreated to the Begijnhof where they devoted their time to prayer, needlework and to nursing patients in the hospitals.

The convent was destroyed by fire several times but was rebuilt each time. The small houses adjoining it were con- structed mainly in the 16th, 17th and 18th centuries. The oldest (at n° 34) is a wooden structure built in 1475. In the middle of the courtyard is a 15th-century church that was transformed into an Anglican Reformed Church in 1607. Opposite is a clandestine Catholic chapel built in 1665.

Use the left-hand door and take the public passageway to the left to reach the **Civic Guard Gallery** *(open Mon-Sat 10am- 5pm, Sun 1-5pm).* This covered street gallery, an annex of the Historical Museum (see 'Museums' section p. 85), exhibits 16th- and 17th-century paintings of the Civil Guards. The most famous, however, is Rembrandt's *Night Watch* in the Rijksmuseum (see p. 88).

▬ *FROM THE KALVERSTRAAT TO THE SINGEL*
I, CD4

Opposite the Civic Guard Gallery, turn right toward the Kalverstraat. Take this street left to n° 156, **Madame Tus- saud's Museum,** which houses a collection of waxwork figures *(open daily 10am-6pm, July 1-Sept 1 until 8pm; f9.50 admission charge).* Here you can see famous politi- cians, artists and athletes surrounded by a multitude of objects, amid a sound-and-light show.

René Descartes (1596-1650)

The great French philosopher and mathematician spent about 20 years of his life in the Netherlands. His stay coincided with the great scientific developments of 17th-century Europe, an epoch of intensive interchange between European scientists and scholars.

He came to the Netherlands looking for a place where he could think and work undisturbed. He had inherited enough money from his father to enjoy an adequate annual income for life.

In Amsterdam, Descartes lived in a gabled house on the Westermarkt, generally spending his days meditating and writing. *Principia Philosophiae*, in which he explained his scientific theories, was written and published in Amsterdam.

He was very attached to the Netherlands, of which he wrote, 'there is no other country where one enjoys such complete liberty, where one can sleep with less uneasiness.'

Back on the Kalverstraat with its shops and cafés, continue until you reach the **Mint Tower** * (Munttoren) I, D4. The Baroque spire was designed by Hendrik de Keyser in 1620; the tower is a vestige of the medieval wall, the Reguliers-poort, built in 1490. In 1692 Louis XIV's armies occupied much of Holland, and the States-General decided as a security measure to transfer the equipment used for minting money from Utrecht to this tower. It has an attractive set of chimes. Concerts are held here in the summer on Friday and Saturday afternoons.

Continue beneath the tower across the bridge to the other side of the Singel, I, D4. This is the first of Amsterdam's great canals, constructed in 1425. On your right is the flower market, or *bloemenmarkt (open Mon-Sat 9am-4:30pm)*. You can buy fresh bulbs, shrubs, dried flowers and even bonsais.

II
THE GOLDEN AGE

With the expansion of its maritime and commercial activity and the influx of refugees from the religious wars (thousands of people from Antwerp, followed by Sephardic Jews and French Huguenots), Amsterdam's population rose from 30,000 to 100,000 people between 1585 and 1620. Enlarging the city thus became an urgent priority. The canals were conceived by the councilmen as part of a comprehensive plan for regional development, largely designed by Hendrick Staets. The **Herengracht** (the Nobles' Canal) was named in honour of the aristocrats who were in power; the **Prinsengracht** (the Prince's Canal), in memory of Prince William of Orange, who led the Dutch rebellion against Spain; and the **Keizersgracht** (the Emperor's Canal), in memory of Austrian Emperor Maximilian I, who added a symbolic crown to the arms of Amsterdam.

The new city was further divided into functional districts: business houses and expensive townhouses were constructed along the canals; more modest dwellings went up on the side streets; warehouses were conveniently located near the port; and the Brouwersgracht area was reserved for industrial sites and buildings devoted to charitable purposes. To the west of the Prinsengracht an overcrowded area developed, full of narrow streets and inexpensive houses. Not part of the original city plan, this area became known as the Jordaan and was settled largely by refugees. To protect its freedom, the city erected a new defensive enclosure: 5 mi/8 km of walls and ramparts surmounted by 26 mills, the **Singelgracht.** Construction began in 1609 and lasted 50 years.

Bankers and other businessmen have replaced the wealthy merchants and burgesses who once occupied the sumptuous dwellings along the three canals. Yet this part of Amsterdam still has the most handsome façades and lovely carefully preserved old houses, sometimes converted into museums. Here you will most readily absorb the atmosphere of Amsterdam's great Golden Age.

This itinerary should take about three hours; add several hours if you want to visit the museums.

▬ *AROUND THE PRINSENGRACHT AND HERENGRACHT* I, B2-3

This itinerary begins in the western section of the city at the Western Church.

Western Church * (Westerkerk) I B2-3

Tours of the towers are given June 1-Sept 15, Tues-Sat 2-5pm.

Erected between 1620 and 1638 according to the plans of Hendrik de Keyser, the Protestant church is a good example of the Dutch Renaissance style. It is one of the architect's masterpieces. The tower is topped by the imperial crown, which Maximilian of Austria authorized Amsterdam to display.

Rembrandt was buried in this church on October 8, 1669, alongside his son Titus and mistress Hendrickje, but the exact location of the painter's tomb is unknown.

There is now a café in what used to be the presbytery. There are a number of fine residences behind the church: Descartes (see p. 66) lived for some time at n° 6 in 1634 during his exile in Holland (the house bears a commemorative plaque).

The Anne Frank House ** I, B3

Open Mon-Sat 9am-5pm, Sun and holidays 10am-5pm; f4 admission charge.

Anne Frank (1929-1945)

Anne Frank, second daughter of Otto Frank and Edith Frank-Holländer, was born in Frankfurt-am-Main on June 12, 1929 during Hitler's rise to power. When Hitler became chancellor in 1933, Jewish shops were boycotted and Jewish officials dismissed. Otto Frank decided not to wait until things became even worse and fled to Amsterdam with his family. In May 1940 the German army invaded the Netherlands, which was forced to capitulate in five days. His experiences in Germany had made Mr Frank wary, and he began to fix up the rear house of his office on the Prinsengracht. Early in July 1942, his eldest daughter, Margot, received a summons to perform compulsory labour. The Frank family decided to move into their hideout without further delay. They were soon joined by two other Jewish families. Anne had just celebrated her 13th birthday. Her present was a diary in which she wrote passages that were destined to become immortal. Koophuis and Kraler, two of Frank's non-Jewish associates, and the two office workers, Miep and Elli, knew of the family's whereabouts. They brought the hidden occupants food, clothing, books and whatever else they needed. Anne continued to fill her journal with page after page of astonishingly mature and sensitive writing. The last entry was made on August 1, 1944. On August 4, a car with German and Dutch policemen drew up before the door. They went immediately to the bookcase and discovered the terrified Frank family. One of the policemen demanded that they hand over their valuables. In order to carry his loot he picked up Mr Frank's briefcase and emptied its contents out on the floor. It contained Anne's journal, which was left lying there while the family and Frank's two associates were taken away. Anne and her sister Margot were transferred to Bergen-Belsen, where they died in March 1945. Only Otto Frank survived the war.

On the advice of some friends, Otto Frank decided to publish the journal that Miep had saved under the title chosen by Anne herself, *The Rear House (Achterhuis)*. Since then it has been published in more than 50 countries and has sold more than 30 million copies. Many stage productions and a film have been based on it.

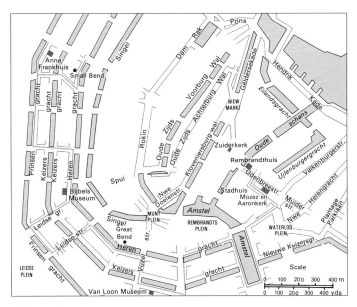

Itinerary II

Heading north along the Prinsengracht, you will come to the Anne Frank House at n° 263. Built in 1635 as an office and warehouse, the building resembles many others in old Amsterdam. Land was expensive along the canals and houses were therefore narrow and deep. In order that the back part could receive the sunlight, a courtyard was constructed and a second house built according to a plan which became typical of Amsterdam's domestic architecture. It was in the rear house that Anne Frank hid from the Germans and wrote the journal which was to make her famous.

The house was saved from demolition through the efforts of the people of Amsterdam and the rear part has been preserved as arranged by Anne's father, Otto Frank. The Frank family and their friends occupied the house from 1942 until they were arrested on August 4, 1944. They spent these 25 months on two floors and in the garret, the entrance to which was concealed by a swinging bookcase. The windows of the house are still shaded and a few yellowing photographs on the faded wallpaper of Anne's room reflect the interests, delights and concerns of a little girl who so poignantly recorded her years in hiding. The Anne Frank Foundation occupies the front house. Its purpose is not only to perpetuate the memory of Anne Frank but to work for a future in which such tragedies will never reoccur.

THE FODOR, VAN LOON AND WILLET HOLTHUYSEN MUSEUMS I, D4-5

From the Prinsengracht, turn right on the Leliegracht and again on the Herengracht. This is known as the **Small Bend ★★**, I, B3. There are some outstanding façades here, including a house with a fine gable and an inscription, *Soli*

deo Gloria (Glory to One God) at n° 168. This is now the
Theatre Museum *(open Tues-Sun 11am-5pm; f2.50 admission charge)*, which contains an extensive collection of
drawings, prints, paintings and sketches for stage settings
and costumes, masks and models. The museum gives a
picturesque overview of Dutch theatre.

The recently restored red and white buildings at n° 170 and
n° 172 are jointly known as the Hotel Bartolotti. They were
designed by Hendrik de Keyser in 1622.

Turn right in Raadhuisstraat and when you reach the Westerkerk, turn left on the Prinsengracht. Turn left again on
Berenstraat (which becomes Wolvenstraat). There are a
number of good restaurants here. When you reach the
Herengracht, turn right.

Further along the Herengracht at n° 366 is the **Bible
Museum ***, I, C3, *(open Tues-Sat 10am-5pm, Sun 1-5pm; f3
admission charge)*. Housed in several beautifully austere
18th-century buildings with lavish façades, the museum is
devoted to various aspects of the Bible: the Exodus, daily life
in biblical times, history of the Bible in Dutch, etc.

Turn right on the Leidsegracht, I, D3. On the corner at n° 394
is a coat of arms depicting the *Four Sons of Aymon* astride a
black charger. The Leidsegracht is distinguished by several
enchanting little 17th-century houses with attractive gables.
Turn left on the Prinsengracht.

There is a series of houses dating from the early 18th century
with gables topped by a semi-circular pediment from n° 681
to n° 693. The vast building that houses the law courts is
opposite, at n° 436. It was built in the neo-Classical style
between 1825 and 1829.

Take Leidsestraat, a shopping street for pedestrians only, to
the left. Then walk to the right along Herengracht. The next
street on the right, Nieuwe Spiegelstraat, is where the finest
and most expensive antique shops are located. On the other
bank of the canal (between Nieuwe Speigelstraat and Vijzelstraat), you will see the **Great Bend ****, I, D3-4, a group of
houses which are among the most opulent in Amsterdam.
The façades are perhaps somewhat austere but they reflect to
perfection the confidence and wealth of the patricians, bankers and traders who gave Amsterdam's Golden Age its
lustre. Notice, for example, the palatial building at n° 475,
erected between 1668 and 1672 for a wealthy merchant.
Return to the Keizersgracht via Vijzelstraat.

Fodor Museum * I, D4

Open daily 11am-5pm; free admission.

On the far side of the Keizersgracht, at 609, is one of the
Netherlands' oldest museums. In 1860 the coal merchant
Carel Joseph Fodor bequeathed his collection of paintings,
engravings and drawings to the city of Amsterdam on condition that his three houses be converted into a museum. It was
opened to the public in 1863.

Today, Fodor organizes exhibitions of contemporary art,
generally by young artists from Amsterdam and its immediate
surroundings. Each year the museum hosts an international
exchange exhibition with a different European capital. Additionally, the Fodor Museum holds an annual display of *objets*

A canal boat is a pleasant way to visit Amsterdam's canals.

d'arts purchased by the city of Amsterdam under a program called 'Amsterdam Purchases Art.'
Cross the bridge on Vijzelstraat to the other side of the Keizersgracht, where the Van Loon Museum is located.

Van Loon Museum I, E4

Open Mon 10am-5pm; f3 admission charge.

Located at Keizersgracht 672, this museum is housed in the original interior of a palatial house built in 1671 by Adriaan Dortsman, one of the most gifted architects of the Golden Age.

The interior is furnished and arranged as it was when the patrician Van Loon family lived there. More than 60 portraits of the Van Loons trace the family's history. You can also see a collection of medals coined for the seven golden-wedding anniversaries celebrated between 1621 and 1722.

There is an attractive French-style garden behind the house. What appears to be an 18th-century temple in fact conceals the former carriage house. Behind it, an alleyway leads to the Herengracht.

Continue east along the Keizersgracht to the Reguliersgracht. The *Hooghoudt* at n° 11 is a magnificent renovated warehouse where people meet to chat and have a drink at the counter among wooden barrels and old bottles. Turn left onto the Reguliersgracht.

This is a pleasant district of renovated houses and 17th-century warehouses. At the corner of the Herengracht, you have a superb view of the six bridges of the Reguliersgracht. Cross the bridge and go right on the odd-numbered bank.

Willet Holthuysen Museum * I, D5

Open Tues-Sat 10am-5pm, Sun and holidays 1-5pm; f1.75 admission charge.

This small historical museum at Herengracht 605 was the home of Jacob Hop and his wife Isabella Hoogt. It was built during the extensive urban construction in the 17th century.

Amsterdam's coat of arms

The imperial crown lies atop Amsterdam's coat of arms, a red escutcheon containing a black pale supporting three white St Andrew's crosses.

In 1489 Maximilian of Austria authorized Amsterdam to display the imperial crown above its coat of arms in recognition of the city's aid to the Burgundian and Austrian princes.

Amsterdam at that time was not an imperial city directly dependent on the emperor. It belonged to the count of Holland. The right to display the imperial crown above its coat of arms was consequently a most exceptional privilege. This right also had practical implications because ships bearing the city's arms were universally regarded as enjoying imperial protection. The pride Amsterdammers felt in this privilege was reflected in the installation, in 1638, of the imperial crown at the summit of the tower (280 ft/85 m in height), which Jacob van Campen designed for the Westerkerk.

Only ten municipalities in the entire Netherlands (out of more than 1000) are entitled to display the imperial crown above their coat of arms.

The St Andrew's crosses in the coat of arms are like the Roman figure X. It was on a cross such as this that St Andrew was martyred. The origin of the red-and-black escutcheon is not certain. As in the arms of Dordrecht and Delft, the pale may represent the water on which the city is located. The St Andrew's crosses are more or less common in the arms of municipalities near Amsterdam and might have been borrowed from the arms of the Persijn family, which owned property in the city in the 13th century. This family, which included several knights, is said to have incorporated St Andrew's crosses in its coat of arms.

The two lions were added to Amsterdam's arms as supporters in the early 16th century.

On March 29, 1947, in recognition of the citizens' attitude during the German occupation (1940-1945), H.M. Queen Wilhelmina granted the City of Amsterdam the right to add the motto *Heldhafting, Vastberaden, Barmhargit* (Heroic, Resolute, Compassionate) to its coat of arms.

The museum documents the opulent way of life of wealthy Amsterdammers in the 18th and 19th centuries. Crystal and porcelain, family portraits, chinoiseries and clocks (still keeping time) are on display.

▬▬ *AROUND WATERLOOPLEIN* I, C5

Head east to the Amstel River, around which Amsterdam was first built. Walk along the Amstel to your right until you reach the first bridge, known as the *Magerebrug,* or thin bridge, constructed in 1671. As you cross it, you'll have a fine view of the river and its countless houseboats.

Immediately after the next bridge you will see the **Waterlooplein,** I, C5 on your right. Here is the recently built Town Hall and adjoining Music Theatre, **Stopera.** Designed in a semicircle for a capacity of 1600, the theatre has exceptional acoustics. It is a showcase for performances by the Netherlands National Ballet and Opera and other national and international theatre and music troupes. Go past the subway station and turn right onto Mr. Visserplein. You are now entering Amsterdam's old Jewish quarter, the Jodenbuurt, largely destroyed by the Nazis during World War II. It is estimated that only 10,000 of the 80,000 Amsterdam Jews who were deported returned alive. The square is named after Mr. Visser – a burgomaster who aided the Jewish population during the occupation.

The Portuguese Synagogue * I, D6

Open Apr-Oct, Sun-Tues except during Jewish holidays; free admission.

The synagogue, which miraculously survived the war, was built with funds supplied by the Portuguese Jewish descendants of those who were expelled from their country during the Inquisition in the 15th and 16th centuries. Built in 1671-1675 by architect Elias Bouwman, it is regarded as the finest synagogue in Holland.

The synagogue has remained virtually unchanged since its construction. It is illuminated by large glass windows. Tall pillars support eight vaulted wooden naves from which great copper candelabra, lit during services, are suspended. The synagogue contains a monumental *hechal* (ark of the Torah) and a copy of Manasse ben Israel's *Holy History,* illustrated by his friend Rembrandt.

Jewish Historical Museum
(Joods Historisch Museum) I, D5

Open daily 11am-5pm; f5 admission charge.

This museum was transferred in 1987 to the new complex on Jonas Daniel Meijerplein, which is built around four restored synagogues in what was once Amsterdam's active Jewish quarter. These include the Grote Sjoel (or great synagogue, at the corner of Nieuwe Amsterstraat), erected in 1770; the adjacent **Drittsjoel** (or third synagogue), built in 1770; behind this, the **Obbene Sjoel** (or second synagogue) constructed in 1686; and the **Neie Sjoel** (or new synagogue), built in 1752. The Yiddish word *shul (sjoel)* in Dutch derives from the German *schule,* or school, and refers to the study of the Torah, an important part of the Jewish religion. You could begin by visiting the recently restored Neie Sjoel, which houses an exhibition concerning Jewish history and religion. Also on display is work by the painter Charlotte Salomon who depicted the life of the synagogue in a thousand gouaches.

The Grote Sjoel is the oldest public synagogue in Western Europe. There is an exhibition of sacred objects including illuminated scrolls, menorahs and a 17th century Ark in white marble. Two ritual baths were recently discovered in the Mikwe during restoration work. The other two synagogues were built because the Neie Sjoel was too small. An extensive multi-media library is open to the public.

There is a café serving Jewish cuisine in the museum complex.

A large statue of the docker Mari Andriessen stands on the Jonas Daniel Meijerplein to commemorate the Amsterdam dockers who went on strike to protest against the deportation of the Jewish population. The square is frequently the starting point for protest demonstrations.

The **Flea Market** on Waterlooplein (open Mon-Sat) offers everything from pianos to books, old postcards, clothes, furniture, bicycles, dolls and glassware. The market came into existence after World War II on the site of the former Jewish trading area.

Also on Waterlooplein is the **Moses and Aaron Church** (Mozes en Aaron kerk), a Jesuit-style Catholic oratory which owes its name to the figures of the two brothers that

Rembrandt Harmenszoon van Rijn (1606-1669)

Rembrandt was born in Leyden, the fourth son of a miller. He received a strict Protestant upbringing in which the Bible played a central role; in keeping with Protestant tradition, wide scope was given to personal interpretation of the Bible, and it remained a deep source of inspiration throughout the artist's life.

At 15, he enrolled in Leyden University to study law and theology but soon left the university and was apprenticed to a local painter. His talent was immediately recognized, and by 1629 Rembrandt had a distinguished patron (as did all Dutch artists of his time): Constantin Huyghens, secretary of state to Prince Frederick Henry of Orange.

In 1631 the artist moved into the house of Hendrick van Ulenborch, a well-known Amsterdam art dealer. He soon married van Ulenborch's 20-year-old cousin Saskia, a lovely woman from a respectable bourgeois family. Amsterdam was then one of the commercial and cultural centres of Europe and an important art market. Though Rembrandt never traveled, through van Ulenborch he saw many important works by classical and contemporary artists, in particular the Renaissance Italian artists.

Rembrandt was unlike any Dutch artist of his day. He refused to be confined to any genre and painted portraits, historical paintings, biblical scenes, landscapes and illustrations of everyday life with an eye to the human spirit and truth of the subject. Art historian Kenneth Clark wrote that 'apart from his immense gifts as a pure painter... he digs down to the roots of life; and he seems to open his heart to us. We have the feeling that he is keeping nothing back.'

His realistic depiction of his subjects sometimes shocked his contemporaries. A painter of his time wrote: 'He did not hesitate to oppose our rules of art, such as anatomy and the proportions of the human body, and the usefulness of classical statues,' adding that Rembrandt 'did not at all know how to keep his station, and always associated with the lower orders.'

Yet Rembrandt's talent was undeniable and throughout his life he remained an admired, if not fashionable, artist. He had many pupils and numerous portrait commissions, though he was often passed over for important commissions in favour of less inspired but more conventional artists.

While he was earning a lot and had an income from Saskia's substantial dowry, Rembrandt was spending beyond his means. He bought a large house on the Jodenbreestraat and had a reputation as an extravagant bidder at auctions where he accumulated antique busts, old weapons and wind instruments, exotic clothing, engravings and artwork to add to his collection. Later, when his debts rose, he was forced to sell all his possessions.

Of Rembrandt's four children born of his marriage to Saskia, only Titus (born in 1641) survived infancy. Saskia herself succumbed to a long illness only ten months after Titus' birth. After Saskia's death, the artist lived with Hendrickje Stoffels, who remained his faithful companion until her death in 1661.

embellish the façade. Above is a large statue the Amsterdammers irreverently call 'the Church's Puppet.' In fact it represents *Melchizedeck*, a biblical king of Jerusalem at the time of Abraham, offering bread and wine as a sacrifice. The building, no longer used for religious services, has become a cultural centre for young people.

To the left of the church once stood the house where Spinoza was born in 1632 (see p. 41). Take the first street on your left after the church and you will come to Jodenbreestraat, which was the heart of the Jewish quarter. At the turn of the century, 95% of the residents on this commercial street were Jewish.

Rembrandt's *Night Watch*.

In 1965 the north side of the street was completely demolished and the little houses were replaced by modern apartment blocks that are now university offices. Isolated in the midst of these is Rembrandt's house.

■■ REMBRANDT'S HOUSE** I, C5

Open Mon-Sat 10am-5pm, Sun and holidays 1-5pm; f2 admission charge.

Rembrandt lived for about 20 years (1639-1660) in this house at Jodenbreestraat n° 4-6. It is a fine two-storey building topped by the gable characteristic of the period. Already well-known and esteemed as an artist, Rembrandt received major commissions but the considerable sum he had paid for the house (13,000 guilders) was to plunge him into serious financial difficulties. In 1657-1658 he had to sell it and all his possessions in order to pay his debts.

The living quarters were on the ground floor. The studio and two rooms containing the artist's paintings and collections were on the floor above. The top floor was a studio for his pupils.

Converted into a museum in 1911 after extensive restoration, the house contains 250 original engravings printed by Rembrandt himself. Among the most famous are *The Three Crosses* (room A), *Christ Presented to the People* (room A), *Rembrandt's Mother* (room C) and various self-portraits (room C). Several portraits of women hang in the first upper room and the famous *Hundred Guilder Print* in the large second-storey room.

Drawings by Rembrandt and paintings by his pupils and teachers, including Pieter Lastman who had a major influence on the artist, are also on display during temporary exhibitions arranged by the museum.

Cross the bridge and turn left, continuing straight along the Zwanenburgwal. Here you can see a typical example of the city's attempt to modernize while maintaining the traditions of Amsterdam architecture. Construction of the subway was responsible for the demolition of many houses here. One of Amsterdam's architects managed to fill the gaps by constructing apartment houses that, while thoroughly modern, do not seem in the least out of place.

Turn back and continue until you reach St Antoniesbreestraat.

Continue straight ahead to the monumental Pinto House (1680) at n° 69. Built for Isaac de Pinto, a Portuguese Jew whose family migrated to Amsterdam in 1492, it was restored in 1975 and is now a public library. Just opposite is the Zuiderkerkhof or Southern Cemetery. The entrance was sculpted in 1612 by Englishman Nicholas Stone, son-in-law of architect Hendrik de Keyser.

Alternatively, turn left off St Antoniesbreestraat onto Nieuwe Hoogstraat and again left on the first street to have a look at the Zuiderkerk. The first church built in Amsterdam after the Reformation, its tower (1614) is the work of Hendrik de Keyser. Rembrandt's first three children were buried here.

III
NORTH-WEST AMSTERDAM:
THE JORDAAN

The area of the city to the west of the Prinsengracht was left out of the plans for the expansion of Amsterdam adopted by the municipal council in 1609. It soon became a crowded semi-slum where the most underprivileged citizens came to live. A maze of narrow streets developed, lined with small houses and intersected by tiny canals.

In the late 17th century, many French Huguenot refugees settled in this area. It was perhaps the French who baptized this labyrinth of streets and canals *le jardin*, or garden, a name later transformed by the Dutch into *Da Jordaan*. Lacking the homogeneity and grandeur of the city centre, it became one of the most animated and colourful neighbourhoods of the city, with its own unique atmosphere and street life.

The residents of the Jordaan are proud of their heritage and have more than once fought controversial urban reconstruction projects. In 1973 the city decided to avoid demolition whenever possible and to concentrate on renovation, while maintaining the balance between houses and businesses typical of this area. The Jordaan today is filled with small boutiques, art galleries, restaurants and cafés (you can find one on almost every corner). It is a favourite haunt of students and artists and retains a distinctive neighbourhood flavour.

This walk takes approximately one and a half hours.

▬ THE JORDAAN ** I, AB2

The best starting point for this walk is the **Westerkerk** (Western Church), I, B3, on the Prinsengracht. Cross the bridge on your left and walk to the right. At n° 180 is the House of Keyser, coffee and tea merchants since 1839. Turn left on Bloemgracht (canal of flowers). Lined with attractive houses, it is sometimes called the 'Herengracht of the Jordaan,' the canal of the Nobles of the Jordaan. There is a pearl shop at n° 38, the *1001 Kralen* or 1001 Pearls. Take the second lane on the right, Tweede Leliedwarsstraat, where the sidewalks are covered with flower tubs to prevent cars from parking. Turn to the left at the first canal, the Egelan-

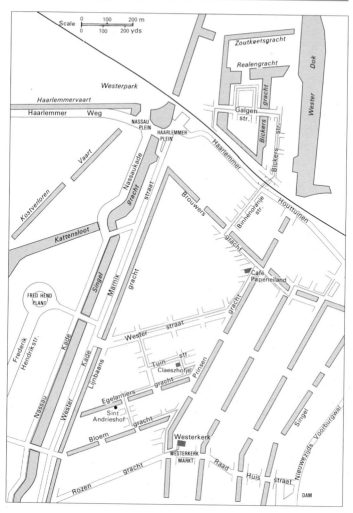

Itinerary III

tiersgracht (the wild rose canal). At n° 107, take the doorway crowned with the words *Sint Andrieshof* into a passageway covered with blue and white Delft tiles, which leads to a little courtyard surrounded by small renovated houses. This *hof*, an almshouse for elderly and needy people, was founded by a priest in 1610.

Turn back and follow the Egelantiersgracht until you come to the Prinsengracht. After crossing the bridge on the left, you might like to drink something at the 'brown café' (see p. 26) on the corner, **'t Smalle**. Pieter Hoppe began distilling here in 1780.

Walk along Eerste Egelantiersdwarsstraat – a very big name for a very small street – and take the first street on your right, Egelantiersstraat. There is another typical *hof*, Claes Claeszhofje, at n° 18-20, founded in 1616 by Claes Claeszoon

Anslo, an Amsterdam cloth merchant. It was rebuilt in the second half of the 17th century and was recently modernized to house students from the Conservatorium.

Cross the building through the three small inner courtyards and you will come to a passageway that leads to Eerste Egelantiersdwarsstraat. Turn left on this street, then take Tweedetuindwarsstraat to the right. This is one of the Jordaan's typical commercial streets with a great many cafés, restaurants and shops, each more unusual than the other. When you reach Westerstraat, a former canal which, unfortunately, was filled in in 1861, turn right. There is a cloth and clothing market here on Monday mornings.

You will soon come to the Noorderkerk erected in 1620 in the form of a Greek cross drawn by architects Hendrik de Keyser and Hendrik Staets. There is an antiques market on Mondays and a bird market on Saturdays in the square. Farm produce is sold on the Noordemarkt on Saturday mornings and there is an extensive Flea Market here on Monday mornings. At n° 34 is one of Jordaan's most well-known brown cafés, the Huysman, now renamed **Hegeraad.**

A small monument in the square honors Multatuli (1820-1887, see p. 44) and depicts his famous characters, Wouterje Pieterse and Femke. The first two buildings you come to along the Prinsengracht are a 1641 café at n° 2, **Papeneiland,** one of the oldest in Amsterdam, and a 1656 shop.

Continue to the left on the **Brouwersgracht ★★** (the Brewers' Canal), I, A3-4, which is one of the most delightful spots in Amsterdam. Old warehouses have been converted into apartments and the barges float motionless on the water.

Window boxes and elegant wrought iron contribute to the charm of the Jordaan.

This canal marks the end of the Jordaan. It would be a pity not to go any farther and we can suggest two possibilities (there is nothing to stop you from following both suggestions!).

▰ PRINSENEILAND ** AND ITS WAREHOUSES
II, A4   ·

Cross the first bridge on the Brouwersgracht, and take
Binnenoranjestraat to the right. Then cross the Haarlemerdijk,
where there are a number of shops, cafés, restaurants and
even a small Art Deco cinema. Go beneath the railway bridge
until you get to the Jonkerplein. Keep going straight ahead
on Grotebiekersstraat which leads to Prinseneiland (Princes'
Island), an artificial island where you should walk to the right.
Then keep going left until you reach the little shipyards and
old warehouses. Some are still used for their original purpose;
others have been converted into homes along the canals
where the ships of the past have been replaced by yachts.
Here perhaps is the part of Amsterdam where you can most
readily imagine the look and the atmosphere of the Amsterdam of old.

▰ HERENMARKT * AND THE COLONIAL
ERA I, A4

Go back to the Papeneiland café, cross the bridge on the
Keizersgracht and proceed straight ahead on the Brouwersgracht. The last part of the canal is the most picturesque. The
house on the corner of the Brouwersgracht and Binnen
Brouwersstraat (to the right) is an admirable example of the
charming homes to be seen in Amsterdam, with its stone
steps, wooden façade, basement and outside stairs.

A little farther on, you will reach a small square: the Herenmarkt. Here you can see the back of the East India House,
now used as a municipal registry office and a people's
university. From 1623 to 1647, this was the head office of the
East India Company. Here, in 1625, the decision was taken to
found New Amsterdam, the forerunner of New York. The
cellars were filled with the treasures of Piet Heyn, Grand
Admiral of the Dutch Fleet. The inner courtyard of this
historic building is well worth a visit (the entrance is on the
right). There is a small fountain topped by a statue of Pieter
Stuyvesant, governor of New Amsterdam, in the centre of the
courtyard.

IV
THE AMSTERDAM SCHOOL
OF ARCHITECTURE

Between 1910 and 1930 an architectural school developed in the city, which became celebrated throughout the world as the Amsterdam School. It was distinguished by fantastic forms dominated by the decorative use of brick. The surprising thing about these 'fairytale castles' with their bright colours is that they were built to house workers. Visitors still come from all over the world to admire these 'dreams in brick.'

Some of the essential features of the Amsterdam School, which will enable you to recognize them at a glance, include: expressive façades decorated with hollow and spherical forms and balconies; an extremely decorative use of yellow, orange and reddish-brown brick; accentuation of vertical and horizontal lines by means of chimneys, balconies and windows; and the application of sculptures (usually in brick) as an integral part of the building. On sunny days the beauty of these buildings is enhanced by shadows. The harmony of the façades is best appreciated from a distance.

Dozens of architects designed buildings in the style of the Amsterdam School in the 1920s and 1930s. Two who achieved an international reputation deserve particular mention: Michel de Klerk (1884-1923) whose Het Schip (the ship) complex in the Spaarndammerbuurt district has become famous, and Pieter Kramer (1881-1961) who designed more than 200 Amsterdam bridges beginning in 1917. The sculptor Hildo Krop (1884-1970) also made a significant contribution to the characteristic appearance of public buildings, residential buildings and bridges in the style of the Amsterdam School.

The following route will take you past the best examples of the Amsterdam School and these three artists. Your walk should take approximately one and a half hours.

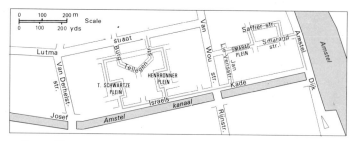

Itinerary IV

■ DE DAGERAAD BUILDING COOPERATIVE
II, E4

Take tram 4 from the centre and get off at Amstel kanaal, at the corner of Van Woustraat and Jozef Israelskade, II, E5 Follow the embankment to the right and then turn to the right on the fourth street, Paletstraat, II, E4. Here you will discover an extensive complex that is considered one of the peak achievements of the Amsterdam School. It was commissioned by the Socialist building cooperative, *De Dageraad*, and built between 1918 and 1923 by de Klerk and Kramer. The complex comprises approximately 350 housing units. Designated an historical monument in 1972, it was recently renovated with exceptional skill, emphasizing the different colours of the brickwork.

The core of this complex is on **Therese Schwartzeplein**, II, E4. The odd-number side is noteworthy for the chimneys and sliding windows designed by de Klerk in accordance with the Amsterdam style.

The buildings continue on the odd-number side of Therese Schwartzstraat. There is a sculpture by Hildo Krop at the corner of this street. Notice the interesting sculptural effect on the façade at n° 13.

Turn to the right on Willem Pastoorsstraat (the name of the cooperative, *Amsterdamse Woningstichting Dageraad*, appears in brickwork above the doors) and then again to the right to reach Burgemeester Tellegenstraat where you will be struck by the undulating line of the roofs. You now come to the most celebrated part of the complex: the two corner buildings near P.L. Takstraat, built between 1921 and 1922. At the corners are brick decorations designed by Hildo Krop and constructed between 1918 and 1923. High up on the façades the name De Dageraad can be seen. The complex, combined with the buildings on P.L. Takstraat, forms an impressive whole. All the characteristic features of the Amsterdam School can be seen here.

There is a simple monument on the little square designed by Kramer in honour of Tellegen (1859-1921), burgomaster of Amsterdam, who encouraged the construction of workers' housing units in the capital. In the background you can see the little tower of the public library.

Continue on Burgemeester Tellegenstraat and you can see that the second part of the complex is a symmetrical reflection of the first. Here, too, the undulating line of the roofs

Former warehouses on Prinseneiland have been converted into apartments.

conceals a sunny terrace. The iron hooks above the windows are used to hoist furniture when new occupants arrive because the stairs are usually too narrow and steep.

Past the street corner on your left, you will see a small doorway leading to the Coöperatiehof. The public library building is topped by a clock tower. The purpose of this building, which symbolizes worker's emancipation, is indicated by an emblematic design over the entrance: a row of books and underneath a key giving access to wisdom, and a serpent twining around the tree of science.

Leave the Coöperatiehof by the same doorway and turn back toward Talmastraat. The architecture on the left-hand side of this street differs considerably from that of de Klerk's complex but belongs nonetheless to the Amsterdam School.

Turn right when you come to Henriëtte Ronnerstraat. The sculpted façades and the decorative use of bricks and tiles are seen again at n° 40 to n° 44.

You now come to Henriëtte Ronnerplein, II, E4, which is the symmetrical counterpart of Therese Schwartzeplein.

■ *EIGENHAARD BUILDING COOPERATIVE* II, E5

Leave de Klerk's and Kramer's great complex by Penseelstraat and turn left on Jozef Israelskade. There is a splendid view of the façades if you follow the path along the water's edge. The buildings along both sides of the canal date from 1920-1930. At the corner of Van Woustraat on the opposite side of the street are two buildings (1923-24) by architect G.J. Rutpers, who was inspired by the Amsterdam School. Cross Van Woustraat and take Jan Lievenstraat to the left. On your right is a somewhat angular variation on the Amsterdam School style. Past Granaatstraat you'll come to a doorway to your right leading to Smaragdplein, II, E5. This has been turned into an urban garden. Most of the buildings in this area were built for the Eigenhaard building cooperative by architect J.C. Van Epen (1880-1960). Streets such as Smaragdstraat (which runs off the square) and Topaasstraat (perpendicular to the square) are especially characteristic of his style. Remarkable public baths (1925) at the end of the Smaragd-plein sports ground are still in use.

Turn to the left on Diamantstraat, II, D5. Here you will see a large housing complex of the Amsterdam School that has recently been renovated. Especially noteworthy are the curved elevator shafts and the wrought-iron service elevator. When you reach Saffierstraat turn to the right. At the end of the street is a sort of belvedere designed by Van Epen for the corner near n° 61-63. Continue along this street and turn to the left on Smaragdstraat toward the Amstel river, where you should again turn to the right.

You will soon reach the bridge over the Amstelkanaal known as the **Berlage Bridge.** This is one of the outstanding bridges of the Amsterdam School and was built by Kramer in 1917. The hexagonal houses at the ends of the bridge are decorated with various brick patterns. Seals sit atop the piles of the bridge. Like many other sculptures in this area the whole work was created by Hildo Krop.

From here return via Jozef Israelskade to your departure point, at the tram 4 stop on Van Woustraat.

MUSEUMS OF AMSTERDAM

You will find more than 30 museums and scores of private collections open to the public, all located within Amsterdam's old defensive walls. Some of the museums that are most representative of the city's art, history and way of life have been mentioned in the course of different itineraries, including: the Netherlands Maritime Museum (see p. 61), the Anne Frank House (see p. 68), the Jewish Historical Museum (see p. 73) and Rembrandt's House (see p. 75).

Three other world-renowned museums – the **Rijksmuseum,** the **Van Gogh Museum** and the **Stedelijk Museum** – are an indispensable part of any visit to Amsterdam. This section describes these and others, both large and small, which will enrich your stay in the city.

A National Museum Pass can be economical if you intend to visit several museums. The pass costs f25 (f12.50 for a youth pass and f17.50 for senior citizens) and will give you free admission to Holland's state museums (350 in all) and to Amsterdam's municipal museums. With the pass you can visit 16 museums in Amsterdam, virtually all of the ones mentioned in this guide. You can purchase a pass at the **Amsterdam Uit Buro,** Leidseplein 26, on the corner of Marnixstraat I, D2, ☎ 21 1211; **VVV,** Stationsplein, opposite the Centraal Station, I, A5, ☎ 26 6444; **VVV,** Leidsestraat 104, I, D2, ☎ 26 6444; or at the entrance to the museums. Bring along a driver's license or passport as identification.

▬▬▬ *RIJKSMUSEUM* ★★★ I, E3

Stadhouderskade 42, ☎ 73-2121; *open Tues-Sat 10am-5pm; Sun and holidays 1-5pm; f6.50 admission charge.*
The Rijksmuseum dates from 1808 when King Louis Napoleon signed a decree for the creation of a great national museum. It was first established in the old town hall, built in the 17th century by Jacob van Campen (now the Royal Palace).

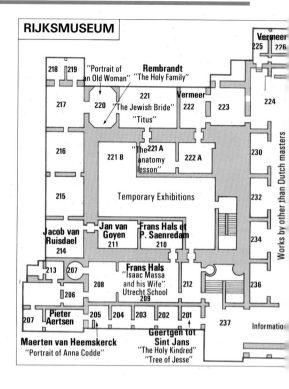

After numerous transfers, the museum found a home in 1885 in the huge building constructed by Petrus J. Cuypers, the architect responsible for Centraal Station (there is, incidentally, a certain similarity between the two buildings). It contains an extensive collection of art from the 15th to the 19th century, in particular almost every major work by the Dutch masters.

The museum comprises five sections: 15th– to 19th– century paintings, sculpture and decorative arts, Dutch history, prints and Asian art.

Ground floor

Department of national history (rooms 101-114)

The country's history since the Middle Ages is illustrated in detail through art, costumes and documents.

Department of Asian art (rooms 12-22)

This section contains works of art from the Far East, with specific exhibits devoted to Indonesia (room 12) and India (room 18). An important collection of Chinese porcelain is in rooms 19-22.

Print room

The museum has an extensive collection of 15th- to 20th-century Dutch drawings and prints, some of which are on display in its changing exhibits. It comprises etchings by Rembrandt, Seghers and Dürer. Temporary exhibits of foreign drawings and prints are also organized. Additionally, the print

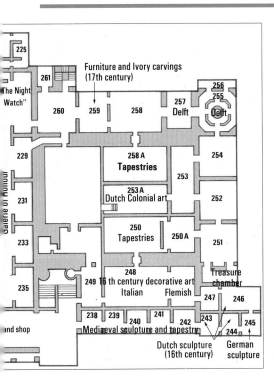

room contains a collection of portraits of famous figures, popular prints and ornamental engravings together with topographic drawings.

18th– and 19th–century Dutch painting (rooms 135-149)

This section contains paintings and some collections of ceramics. *The Regents of the Almoner's Orphanage in Amsterdam,* a work by Cornelis Troost, one of the outstanding Dutch painters of the 18th century, is in room 136.

In *Raampoortje in Amsterdam,* Wouter van Troostwijk depicted Amsterdam at the beginning of the 19th century (room 143). Room 149 contains works by such Amsterdam Impressionists as G.H. Breitner and Isaac Israëls.

Room 138 is reserved for Islamic art and includes some splendid carpets and ceramics.

First floor

15th century: end of the Middle Ages (rooms 201 and 202)

Art in this period commonly depicted religious and biblical themes. The most representative painter of the era is Geertgen tot Sint Jans, whose *Holy Kindred* ★★ and *Adoration of the Magi* ★ can be seen in room 201. Jan Mostaert's *Adoration of the Magi* ★★★ and *Portrait of a Woman* ★ are displayed in the Mostaert room. You can also see the *Seven Works of Mercy* by the Anonymous Master of Alkmaar.

16th century: Renaissance and Mannerism (rooms 203-207)

A little less than a century after its emergence in Italy, the Renaissance made itself felt in Holland. Exclusively religious art was succeeded by mythological representations. The elegant painter Jacob Cornelisz van Oostsanen introduced new elements with *Saul and the Witch of Endor* (room 203) and Lucas van Leyden revealed a marvelous sense of composition and a vivid and expressive technique in his *Triptych with the Adoration of the Golden Calf* ★ (room 204). The influence of the Italian Renaissance on Jan van Scorel, the first Dutch artist to visit Italy, is apparent in his *Mary Magdalene* (room 205). In room 206 you will see the famous *Bathsheba at her Bath* by Cornelis Cornelisz. 'Bourgeois realism' is represented by Pieter Pietersz's *Six Wardens of the Drapers' Guild*. Another noteworthy painting is the *View of a Village on a River* ★★★ by Bruegel the Elder (room 207).

'The Night Watch'

The Night Watch is Rembrandt's largest surviving painting and one of his masterpieces. Originally entitled *The Militia Company of Captain Frans Banning Cocq,* it became popularly known as *The Night Watch* when its varnish darkened in the 19th century.

Rembrandt received the commission to paint the group portrait in 1642. It was common practice at the time for Dutch guilds and companies to commission such portraits. Each member would pay a subscription fee that often determined his prominence in the composition.

All of the well-known artists of the period had done at least one such painting. The result was usually a static composition resembling a series of individual portraits placed side by side. *The Night Watch,* like Rembrandt himself, was completely out of the ordinary.

The scene is painted in the style of the great historical or biblical works of the Renaissance, depicting what appears to be an event of monumental proportions. Captain Cocq (in black in the foreground) and all the militia members are present, and Rembrandt has painted each with his usual insight, intelligence and deep feeling for humanity.

Yet there is more: a dog barking at the sound of a drum; outsiders looking on or swept into the movement; and, above all, a young girl who – without any apparent reason for being there – holds centre-stage along with the captain and Lieutenant van Ruytenburch.

The finished work was placed alongside the other group portraits in the Great Hall of the Kloveniersdoelen, the headquarters of the civic guard. Captain Cocq liked the result enough to have a watercolour reproduction made of it for his personal collection.

In 1715 it was moved to Amsterdam's Town Hall and more than a seventh of the left side of the canvas was cut (including two figures) so that it would fit between two windows. From copies made of the painting, we know that in the original the captain is about to step into the exact vertical centre of the composition, which runs from the right side of his body (the viewer's left) up to the middle of the large archway in the background.

The cut undoubtedly impaired the picture's balance, especially important for an artist who composed his paintings so carefully.

Art historian Kenneth Clark termed the painting 'an extraordinary tour de force,' adding: 'To paint on such a scale without a single dull patch, to keep the figures on the move and yet achieve a stable composition, is evidence of the highest pictorial skill and the result of deep study.'

17th century: The Golden Age (rooms 208-236)

Dutch painting took on a distinctive national character during this period when the country's maritime, political and commercial power was at its height. As a rule, painters specialized in a particular genre: landscapes, still lifes or portraits. The superb portraits of Frans Hals (1580-1666) and W.J. van den Valckert are displayed in rooms 208 and 209. There are also a number of landscapes, among them Jan van Goyen's *Landscape with Two Oaks* ** (room 211) and *The Windmill at Wijk bij Duurstede* ** (room 214) by Jacob van Ruisdael (1628-1682), who is regarded as the greatest landscape painter of the period. Rooms 216-219 are devoted to artists who specialized in depicting everyday life, such as van Ostade and Jan Steen, and some who painted animals, such as Paulus Potter and Albert Cuyp.

Beginning with room 220 you will find paintings from Rembrandt van Rijn's early period. The artist's taste for chiaroscura is already noticeable in the *Portrait of an Old Woman* *** (thought to be his mother reading a book). Certain highlights of his career are on display in room 221, including *The Jewish Bride* ***, *The Syndics* *** and a portrait of his son, *Titus* **. *Nachtwacht* *** *(The Night Watch)*, one of Rembrandt's most famous works, may be seen in room 224. A few steps up will bring you to room 226, with its display of such foreign masters as Fra Angelico, Goya and Rubens. Other paintings by Rembrandt, including his *Self-Portrait as St Paul* **, may be seen in room 229.

Room 232 contains four Jan Vermeer (1632-1675) masterpieces, *The Kitchen Maid* ***, *Woman Reading a Letter* ***, *The Narrow Street* *** and *The Love Letter* ***.

Rooms 233-236 are devoted to some of Rembrandt's contemporaries and pupils, among them Ferdinand Bol, Nicolaes Maes and Aert Gelder, all of whom were profoundly influenced by their master.

Department of decorative arts and sculpture (rooms 238-258)

This department is noteworthy for its magnificent medieval Dutch, Flemish and Germanic sculptures (rooms 238-242), among them *The Death of the Virgin* ** by Adriaen van Wezel of Utrecht (room 242). There is also a splendid collection of tapestries (rooms 243, 248 and 258) and furniture in precious woods (rooms 251-255). You'll find a major collection of delftware displayed in rooms 255-257.

▄▄▄ *VAN GOGH MUSEUM* *** I, F2

Paulus Potterstraat 7, ☎ 76 4881; *open Tues-Sat 10am-5pm, Sun and holidays 1-5pm; f6,50 admission charge.*

The Van Gogh Museum can be reached from the Rijksmuseum through an underground passage for cyclists and pedestrians.

The Van Gogh Museum was opened in 1973 with plans to acquire the works of Van Gogh, his contemporaries and other artists, as well as extensive documentation (there are, for

Vincent Van Gogh (1853-1890)

Undoubtedly the greatest Dutch painter of the 19th century, Vincent Van Gogh's major contribution to modern art was an exploration of the human soul through the use of colour.

His father was a Protestant preacher and gave Vincent a strong Christian upbringing. Vincent saw himself as destined to fulfil God's work by helping people. He came to Amsterdam in May 1877 to prepare for an examination to begin theological studies.

His work with the church was short-lived; sent on a charitable mission to the miners in the Borinage district of Belgium, he angered the evangelist committee by following Christ's teaching too literally: Van Gogh simply gave away all his possessions.

Although he had been drawing for some time, in 1880 he began to take painting very seriously. Returning to his family home in Brabant, he produced his first great paintings, including *The Potato Eaters*. He moved to Paris in 1886 and met some of the most influential Impressionist painters of the time, including Pissarro and Bernard. He also became friends with Paul Gauguin, who later joined him in Arles for several months.

In Arles, Van Gogh developed his use of explosive and vibrant colour. Yet his life became increasingly difficult; his precarious physical and emotional condition deteriorated and his last few months in southern France were spent in the mental hospital of Saint Rémy. He returned to Paris in May 1990, and remained under the care of Dr. Gachet until his death several months later.

Van Gogh's ten years of work, during which he created close to 800 paintings, provide an emotional autobiography. His anguish, solitude and yearning for contact and understanding are manifested in his dramatic, sometimes violent, use of colours and forceful outlines. 'Colour is an expression in itself,' he wrote to his brother Theo; and on another occasion he explained that he had used red and green in a particular painting 'to try to express man's terrible passions.'

To Vincent, the artistic expression of internal emotions came instinctively: 'I did not need to go out of my way to try to express sadness and extreme loneliness,' he wrote of *Wheat Field and Crows*, which he painted in the final months of his life. On July 27, 1890, he shot himself, putting an end to his loneliness and to the brilliant career of an artist who, through his unique genius, left a lasting imprint on modern art.

example, 700 manuscript letters). Today it possesses the world's largest collection of works by Van Gogh – paintings not only from his Dutch period (characterized by their somewhat sombre atmosphere and dark tones) but also from the post-1886 period when Van Gogh had encountered the Impressionists and adopted a range of clear and luminous colours. There are some 200 paintings and 500 sketches and drawings by the artist.

The museum is designed to help the visitor obtain as clear an image of the artist as possible. This framework extends to the periods both before and after Van Gogh, thus giving the viewer an insight into the artists who influenced his work and Van Gogh's effect on other artists.

Van Gogh was also a passionate collector, and the museum exhibits his Japanese prints, magazine illustrations and books.

Van Gogh's own paintings are presented in chronological order and, in part, according to the themes treated. The first floor displays works produced between 1880 and 1886. The second floor is devoted to paintings from 1888 to 1890, the

The elegant façade of the Van Loon Museum.

year of his death. The paintings from his Paris period (1886-1888) serve as a link between the two. The third floor features a selection of the museum's vast collection of Van Gogh's drawings as well as Japanese prints from his personal collection. Finally, on the fourth floor are Van Gogh's canvases, grouped according to subject, together with works by contemporaries such as Bernard, Gauguin, Monticelli and Toulouse-Lautrec, who were held in great esteem by both Vincent and his brother Theo.

The highlight of your visit will undoubtedly be the artist's most famous works: *The Potato Eaters* ★★★, *Self-portrait* ★★★, *Boats on the Beach* ★★, *The Harvest* ★★, and *Wheat Field and Crows* ★★★. The ground floor contains paintings by artists who were friends and contemporaries of the Van Gogh brothers – Laval, Bernard, Corcos, Russel, Lépène, Toulouse-Lautrec and Gauguin – and the superb portrait of Van Gogh by Gauguin, *Vincent Van Gogh Painting Sunflowers* ★★ (1888).

The museum is organized chronologically; paintings and drawings are described according to the place and year in which Van Gogh created them.

Drente (September-November 1883)

During this early period in Van Gogh's career, the artist concentrated on rural motifs, the village peasants, their cottages and their work.

Nuenen (1884-1885)

Van Gogh returned to his family home at Nuenen, in Brabant, where his father had been appointed minister. For two years he worked on paintings and drawings of landscapes, peasants and weavers, producing his first great masterpiece: *The Potato Eaters* ★★★. Describing the painting in a letter to his brother Theo, Vincent wrote: '... those people, eating potatoes in the lamplight, have dug the earth with those very hands they put in the dish, and so it speaks of manual labour, and how they have honestly earned their food.' There are some 50 studies, drawings and sketches for this painting. From this same period, you can also see *The Nuenen Church Door, Cottage at Nightfall, The Nuenen Presbytery, Woman in Red Bonnet, Still Life with Potatoes* and *Four Birds' Nests.*

Antwerp (1885-1886)

Conflicts with the priest and the people of Nuenen made it impossible for him to find models and he therefore set out for Antwerp. 'I imagine it will be good weather this winter on the snow-clad docks,' he wrote to his brother Theo. He was happy at this time, and his palette became more luminous: 'Antwerp is made up of wonderful colours and for that alone it is worthwhile...' Interesting paintings from this period include: *Antwerp Seen from the Painter's Studio, The Quay in Antwerp, Head of Old Man Looking to the Left* and *Portrait of a Woman with Blue Background.*

Paris (1886-1888)

During this period Van Gogh came to know the work of the Impressionists, in particular Monet and Degas. He also met Pissarro, Bernard, Toulouse-Lautrec and Gauguin. He painted landscapes but also portraits: *The Slippers* ★★, *Still Life with Lemons* ★★, several views of Paris, *Still Life with Books* ★★ and the famous *Self-Portrait in Straw Hat* ★★★.

Arles (1888-1889)

His stay in Paris was particularly rewarding both in terms of the development of his style and use of colour. Yet he soon felt the need for a more peaceful place where he could absorb his new discoveries and where it would be warm enough to work outdoors all year round. In February 1888 he went south to Arles in Provence where he lived in the 'Yellow House' not far from the station. He dreamed of founding a community of painters and invited Gauguin to live with him. The visit proved disastrous: tension developed between the two painters and in a moment of rage, Van Gogh threatened Gauguin with a knife and subsequently mutilated his own ear. Above all during this period, Van Gogh worked frenetically and enthusiastically, painting close to one painting every day. He depicted landscapes and still lifes in dazzling light and colour. This period is represented by *Vincent's House in Arles* ★★, *Sunflowers* ★★★, *The Sower* ★★, *The Zouave* ★★★ and *Gauguin's Armchair* ★★.

Saint-Rémy (1889-1890)

In May of 1889, Van Gogh voluntarily committed himself to a mental hospital in Saint-Rémy. The wonderful landscape around the old convent where the hospital was located stimulated the artist's imagination. He wrote to his brother that each painting he did was a 'cry of anguish.' The most noteworthy paintings include: *The Cypresses* ★, *Iris* ★★, *Vincent's Bedroom in Arles* ★★ (painted from memory) and *Three Olive Trees* ★★★.

Auvers (1890)

While Van Gogh was slowly recovering from his breakdown, his paintings began to receive some recognition from fellow artists in Paris. In May 1890 he left Provence for Auvers-sur-Oise, where Dr. Paul Gachet looked after him with great care. In spite of this, and possibly because he was fearful of a relapse, Van Gogh shot himself on July 27, 1890. He died on July 29 and was buried in the cemetery of Auvers-sur-Oise in the middle of the wheat fields. His brother Theo survived him by only six months and was buried by his side. Paintings from this period include: *View of Auvers* ★, *The Château of Auvers* ★, *Field Beneath a Stormy Sky* ★★ and *Wheat Field and Crows* ★★★, one of Van Gogh's last works.

Completing the Museumplein complex, adjacent to the Van Gogh museum, you'll find the third of Amsterdam's great museums, the Stedelijk Museum.

▬ *STEDELIJK MUSEUM* ★★★ I, F2

Paulus Potterstraat 13, ☎ 573 2911 or 573 2737; *open daily 11am-5pm; f5 admission charge.*

This museum was designed from the outset as an institute of contemporary art and over recent years has become one of the world's most active centres of avant-garde art. The collections are constantly being expanded. The museum's policy is to concentrate on particular artists rather than to illustrate every possible trend; Dubuffet, Malevitch and De Kooning are among the artists whose work is solidly represented.

About 20 temporary exhibitions each year make it possible to follow the evolution of contemporary artistic expression in painting, sculpture, prints and the applied arts. Permanent exhibitions, with works displayed in rotation, feature artists such as Chagall, Monet, Cézanne, Mondrian and the German Expressionist painters. The museum also presents the work of various other artistic movements: COBRA (see p. 96), New Realism, American Pop Art, Minimal Art and Conceptual Art.

The Stedelijk is also the crossroads for a wide range of activities in the realm of the plastic arts, not to mention the cinema and modern music. Museum visitors can enjoy free concerts every Saturday from September to June as part of the Music Today series.

Exhibition halls are on the ground floor, along with the restaurant, the international library *(open Mon-Fri 11am-5pm),* with its collection of books on modern art since 1860, and the video room. Catalogues from around the world, newspaper clippings, periodicals and books devoted to artists and artistic trends can be consulted in the library. There you'll also find the latest magazines and full documentation on the exhibitions (the library does not lend books but photocopies are permitted). The Print Room on the mezzanine also has a reading room *(open Mon-Fri 2-5pm or by appointment).* The restaurant in this museum has become a favourite meeting place in Amsterdam. Enjoy a cup of coffee here while admiring the sculptures in the garden facing you.

Painting department
The beginning of modern art is well represented with work by artists such as Vincent Van Gogh, including his well-known *Self-Portrait in Grey Hat* ** and *The Rocking Chair* *. Other artists include Paul Cézanne, Claude Monet, Pablo Picasso, Max Ernst and Georges Braque. Marc Chagall is well represented with paintings such as *The Violinist* ** and *The Pregnant Woman* *. On the first floor is a gouache by Matisse, *The Siren and the Parrot* **.

German Expressionism
Work by German artists from before World War I to the early 1930s is displayed in this room. With the growth of Nazism, many of the artists chose exile or were forced to accept the academic art imposed by the regime. The museum's collection includes paintings by Wassily Kandinsky, Oskar Kokoschka, Paul Klee and Max Beekman.

De Stijl
The artists representing this Dutch abstract movement include Piet Mondrian, who aimed for a maximum degree of purity and clarity through abstraction. Works by Van Doesburg and Gildewart are also represented in this part of the museum.

Malevitch
The Malevitch exhibition surveys the development of this artist born in Russia in 1878. After producing paintings influenced by Fauvism and Cubism, Malevitch began to use simple geometric forms: circles, crosses and rectangles. With these elements he created precise and austere works that represent one of the earliest stages of what was to become Constructivism.

COBRA
The movement's main works on display here are by Karel Appel, Pierre Alechinsky and Pieter Ouborg. You can also see a fresco by Appel in the restaurant.

American Pop Art
The museum's collection of pop artists includes works by Jasper Johns, Roy Lichtenstein and Claes Oldenburg. A painting by Californian artist Edward Kienholz is displayed on the ground floor.

De Stijl

Between World War I and World War II, Dutch art was dominated by the De Stijl (The Style) movement. It took its name from the magazine founded and edited by artist Theo Van Doesburg in 1917.

An informal group of painters, designers and architects gathered around the magazine whose goal, as its editor formulated it, was 'to pave the way for a deeper artistic culture... based on a pure equivalence between the age and its means of expression.' Other than Van Doesburg, Dutch artists who belonged to the movement included Gildewart and van der Leck but its foremost representative was the father of neo-plasticism, Piet Mondrian.

Mondrian, an established artist at the time, was greatly influenced by Cubism during his increasingly frequent stays in Paris (beginning in 1912). He felt, however, that Cubism was not going far enough '... it was not developing towards its own goal, the expression of pure plastic form.'

In the first issue of *De Stijl,* Mondrian wrote that plasticism (the Dutch word *beelding* means generation of form) is the necessary corollary of the modern artist's recognition that 'the emotion of beauty is cosmic, universal.' 'The new plastic idea,' he affirmed, 'cannot, therefore, take the form of a natural or concrete representation... it should find its expression in the abstraction of form and colour, that is to say, in the straight line and the clearly defined primary colour.'

American Action Painting

This style of painting developed after World War II when the influx of European artists to America (especially New York) contributed to the explosive growth of American art. Among these artists are Jackson Pollock and Willem de Kooning.

New Realism

This exhibition groups the trends in Europe in the early 1960s that were concerned with depicting everyday objects. It includes works by Yves Klein, Niki de Saint-Phalle and Tinguely.

Department of Applied Arts

This section comprises industrial design, typography and applied arts such as ceramics, furniture design, textiles and objects in glass, wood or metal. Don't miss the collection of posters (approximately 20,000), the furniture (especially the work of Gerrit Rietveld) and the monumental textiles.

Department of Engravings, Drawings and Photographs

The Print Room located on the mezzanine organizes temporary exhibitions of works by the COBRA group, Picasso, Kandinsky, Klee, Malevitch, Chagall and Dutch artists such as Heyboer and Lucebert.

Sculpture department

Part of the museum's sculpture collection is on permanent display in the garden, in front of the new wing on Van Baertestraat. It includes works by Moore, Renoir, Serra, Rodin, Duchamp and Arp, among others.

After visiting the museum, there is no better way to relax than by taking a stroll through nearby **Vondelpark.** In the 1960s and 1970s, the park was used as an open-air dormitory for thousands of hippies.

COBRA

In the wake of World War II, young Dutch artists were looking for a new form of artistic expression appropriate to post-war realities. Three of them, Constant, Appel and Corneille, worked with Belgian and Danish colleagues to form a group called COBRA. Its name was derived from the initial letters of the capitals Copenhagen, Brussels and Amsterdam, and it had a violent and primitive sound to it that suited the group's artistic ideas.

'We are entering a new era in which the entire cultural pattern of conventions will lose its meaning,' wrote Constant in 1948, 'and in which it will be possible to create a new freedom out of the most primary source of life.'

Inspired by Dadaism, Expressionism and primitive art, COBRA was opposed to geometric abstraction and French traditionalism. They painted in aggressive, vivid colours and sweeping forms 'like a barbarian in a barbarous age,' according to Appel.

In the words of Constant's 1948 manifesto: 'A painting is no longer a construction of colours and lines, but an animal, a night, a cry, a man, or all of these together. Suggestion is boundless, and that is why we can say that, after a period in which art represented nothing, art has now entered a period in which it represents everything.'

In addition to COBRA members in Holland, Asger Jorn, Alechinsky and Christian Dotremont were among its more remarkable painters. Their first exhibition as a group, held at the Stedelijk Museum in 1949, provoked a scandal. Appel's technique of using inches-thick paint on his Abstract Expressionist painting was labeled 'barbaric' by critics.

During the following two years other COBRA exhibitions were held in Europe, especially in Paris, and ten issues of a COBRA revue were published. The group was formally dissolved in 1951 in order to avoid stylistic rigidity. By this time some of its members had gained international renown and continued individually to create passionate, imaginative paintings.

COBRA's post-war Expressionism had a notable influence on Dutch art in the 50s. Paintings of the group can be viewed in the Stedelijk Museum and Amsterdam's major art galleries.

It is a superb park, almost 1 mi/1.5 km long, with splendid trees on lavishly green lawns, lakes dotted with islets and fountains that are illuminated in summer. There is a monument in honour of the great 17th-century Dutch poet Joost van den Vondel (1587-1679, see p. 61). Concerts, dance performances and plays are held in the park during the summer.

▬ *HISTORICAL MUSEUM* ** (AMSTERDAMS HISTORISCH MUSEUM) I, C3

Kalverstraat 92. Open Tues–Sat 10am-5pm, Sun and holidays 1-5pm.

This superb group of buildings dates from the 15th century when St Lucian's Cloister was founded here. In 1578 the city joined forces with William of Orange against Spain, and ownership of the convent passed into the hands of the municipal authorities who decided to convert it into an orphanage. The small doorway with its elaborate decoration dates from this period; it is the work of Joost Jansz. In 1632 the city architect, Pieter de Keyser, constructed the elegant arcade joining the Kalverstraat to the inner courtyard of the girls' section. Two years later, a new wing separating the interior courtyard into two parts was built by Jacob van Campen. Finally, in the 18th century, a plan drawn up by

Hendrik de Keyser was implemented, giving the building a symmetrical wing.

Restored and organized as a museum in 1969, this is now one of the country's finest and largest museums both in terms of its collections and the exhibitions.

You enter from the girls' courtyard. In this wing, the museum has organized a permanent exhibition covering Amsterdam's history from the 13th to the late 19th century. The boys' wing (you will have noticed in the courtyard the huts where the orphans kept their tools) is used for temporary exhibitions.

Amsterdam's origins (rooms 1-2)

These rooms display a number of maps and engravings, which show the original city plans, as well as the first official city document, a letter dated October 17, 1275, signed by Floris V, Count of Holland. Several paintings depict the early city architecture, and you can see a reconstructed kitchen from this era, complete with several recently discovered objects: kitchen utensils, tableware, shoes and buckles.

Trade and industry (rooms 3-5)

The 14th and 15th centuries were a period of rapid growth for Amsterdam. The city itself was expanding according to well-determined plans, and its position as an international trading power was firmly established. These rooms display various crafts of the era, including the manufacture of woolen goods and leather work. You'll find portraits here of the various kings and counts and several interesting views of the city. Room 5 is devoted to Amsterdam's relationship with the sea, particularly navigation, exploration and trading in the East Indies, China and the Baltic Sea. Amsterdam became an important centre for map-making during this period.

The Golden Age (rooms 6-11)

Wealth, tolerance and growth are the key words of this period in Amsterdam's history. Models representing the most important buildings of the time reflect the city's position as an international economic power. Note the model of the East India Company building and those of several canal homes used as warehouses. A slide projection shows the opulence of Amsterdam's burghers and how they lived behind the narrow façades of the canal houses.

This period was also marked by the cultural development in the city. The tremendous prosperity attracted artists from all over Europe. The museum displays paintings by Ferdinand Bol, Jacob Ruisdael and Jan van der Heyden.

Religious tolerance was an important ideal in 17th- and 18th-century Amsterdam. This section features displays of the city's various churches and a portrait of Descartes by an unknown artist.

Room 11 is devoted to the charitable institutions and benefactors who worked to improve the lot of Amsterdam's poor and orphans.

18th century (rooms 12-15)

Amsterdam's position as a trading power began to wane in this century, and there was a decline in the city's industrial activities. There was, however, an increased diversification and refinement in the arts, as illustrated by several splendid objects from the period. Note the painting and panel by Jacob de Wit. The collections of Clubs and Academies founded during the Age of Enlightenment also feature some interesting items, for example sculptures by Adriaen de Lelie. Rooms 13 and 14 display jewelry, furniture and examples of the famous Amstel porcelain.

19th-20th centuries (rooms 16-17)

Room 16 exhibits the plans and construction of the canal linking the city to the North Sea, and there are several paintings of sailors. Commerce is represented with examples of the tobacco and coffee trades.

Room 17 is devoted to various aspects of the 20th century: the depression of the 1930s, the war years, urban development and the evolution of the different city areas, and the unique era of the 1960s.

Room 18 is devoted to temporary exhibitions and prints; room 19 is a public library *(open Tues-Sat 1-5pm)*.

A relief sculpture at the Historical Museum with the inscription 'In the Old Walls'.

■ OTHER MUSEUMS

Allard Pierson Museum ** I, C4

Oude Turfmarkt 127, Rokin 44, ☎ 525 2556; *open Tues-Fri 10am-5pm, Sat, Sun and holidays 1-5pm; f2.50 admission charge.*

Founded in memory of the 19th-century humanist Allard Pierson, this is the archaeological museum of the University of Amsterdam. It exhibits Egyptian, Greek, Etruscan and Roman antiquities, as well as archaeological finds from West Asia, Mesopotamia, Iran, Cyprus, the Cycladic Islands and Mycenae. The museum is housed in the former building of the Nederlandsche Bank.

The ground floor is primarily devoted to Egyptian antiquities from 5000 BC to AD 500. The collection includes vases, jewelry, mirrors, and bronze items. Room 3 contains some interesting wax paintings produced in Fayum between AD 200 and AD 500. The other areas represented include Asia Minor, Mesopotamia and Iran (from the prehistoric period to the end of the Sassanian era, circa AD 651). Room 6 contains sculpture from Greece and Cyprus; of particular interest are the two 6th-century BC stone busts from Cyprus, which reflect a dual Greek and Assyrian influence.

Coptic (Egyptian Christian) sculpture and textiles, from AD 451 to the Arab conquest in AD 641, are displayed in room 7.

On the upper floor, rooms 8 to 14 are devoted to Greek antiquities. You'll find an interesting collection of vases, from the geometric period through black- and red-figure vases, including an Attic cup showing the figure of Hercules (late 6th century BC) and a Roman sculpture modeled after a 4th-century BC Greek work.

Greek ceramics and sculpture from the Hellenistic period (late 4th to 2nd century BC) are well represented, with works that include a noteworthy bronze mirror and admirable Tanagra statuettes and antefixes (roof ornaments placed above a cornice).

Rooms 15 and 16 display Etruscan jewelry, glassware and funerary objects from the 2nd century BC. Don't miss the stone Sphinx head (circa 530 BC), an Etruscan votive monument with archaic-style bas-reliefs (circa 500 BC) and the admirable collection of Etruscan ceramics.

Finally, room 17 is devoted to Roman sculptures. Works here include a bust of Hermaphrodite (AD 200) and a fine bust of a child, possibly a grandson of Emperor Augustus, dating from the reign of Augustus (31 BC-AD 14).

Tropical Museum ⋆ (Tropenmuseum) II, C6

Linnaeusstraat 2, ☎ 568 8200; *open Mon-Fri 10am-5pm, Sat, Sun and holidays noon-5pm; f4.50 admission charge.*
Life in the tropics comes alive here through a multi-media exhibit including slides, video and music. The vivid displays are organized by continent – Asia and Oceania are on the first floor, with Africa, Latin America and the Middle East on the second – and by theme, such as clothing, music or environment.

The exhibits will give you an idea of life in an Arab street or African market through re-creation of the scenes using authentic material and objects. The richness and diversity of the cultures and contemporary problems are explored in depth in an extremely interesting way that makes the museum a pleasure for both adults and children.

Artis Museum-Zoo ⋆ II, C5-6

Plantage, Kerklaan 38-40, ☎ 26 2833; *open daily 9am-5pm; f1 admission charge.*
Artis, founded in 1838, is the oldest zoo in the Netherlands. Its home is a superb garden in the centre of Amsterdam's Plantage, an elegant residential district. In the 20th century it

expanded its original aim – to disseminate knowledge of natural history – and now endeavours to protect and preserve flora and fauna in their natural habitat.

Artis has 6000 animals, including 2000 fish in the country's largest aquarium. There is a huge pool where visitors can watch sea lions at play. A new Planetarium (opened in 1988) and a restaurant are also in the grounds.

University Botanical Gardens (Hortus Botanicus)
I, D6

Plantage Middenlaan 2, ☎ 522 2405; *open Mon-Fri 9am-4pm, Sat, Sun and holidays 11am-4pm; f2.50 admission charge.*

The botanical gardens, originally established in 1682 as a medicinal herb garden, contain more than 6000 plant species from virtually every country in the world. In addition to the many visitors who come here to take advantage of the beautiful surroundings, the gardens are used by Amsterdam University for teaching and research.

ENVIRONS OF AMSTERDAM

Merchant ships and fishing vessels no longer sail the Zuiderzee – the Southern Sea. It ceased to exist on May 28, 1932, at precisely 1:12pm, when the last opening of the Great Dike was filled in. About 500,000 acres of land were recovered from the sea, and the only sails you can see here nowadays are those of private yachts on Lake IJssel.

From Amsterdam, it's easy to visit several former fishing villages to the north-east – Marken, Monnickendam and Volendam – which are thriving towns, thanks to a busy tourist trade. The charming town of Edam, located to the north, is well worth a day's excursion.

The historical towns of Muiden and Naarden, both also easily accessible on a day's excursion, are east of Amsterdam. Above all, don't miss a visit to Haarlem for its historical and artistic treasures.

For an explanation of hotel classifications and a price guide, see the section 'Amsterdam Addresses' p. 117.

▬ *MONNICKENDAM* ★★

By bus, take NZH n° 111 in front of the St Nicholas Church; by road, leave Amsterdam by the S 11 and the IJtunnel. Monnickendam is a small port 7.4 mi/12 km north-east of Amsterdam on the edge of the Gouwzee opposite the island of Marken. The two towns have always been rivals, the former Catholic and the latter fiercely Protestant.

It was founded in the 13th century by Frisian monks who walled in a small lake from the sea. This is probably the origin of the name, the 'monks' dike.'

Start at the **St Nicholas Church** or **Grote Kerk** *(open June 15-Aug. 15, Mon-Sat 10:30am-12:30pm, 2-4pm, Sun 2-4pm)*.

It was built in 1420 in the Gothic style. It has a tower 181.5 ft/55 m high and now belongs to the Reformed Church. Note the choir screen (1562) in carved wood, an organ in the Gothic style, and superb vaults on the three naves.

Leaving the church, take the main street, Noordeinde, lined with small houses ornamented with gables and coats of arms, until you reach **Speeltoren.** The old town hall tower (1591) has chimes that are accompanied by animated figures: with the striking of the hour small knights circle around and an angel blows a trumpet. It is now a museum *(open June 15-Aug 31, Mon-Sat 10:30am-4pm, Sun 1-4pm; Sept 1 to June 14, Sat, Sun only).*

The ground floor is devoted to Monnickendam's past (ceramics, tiles, everyday objects, boat models) and the floor above to temporary exhibitions concerning the town.

Opposite the museum at Noordeinde n° 5 is the town hall *(visit by appointment),* which was built in the 17th century as a private home. The gable bears the emblem of Monnickendam, a monk. Follow the road toward the canal, which leads to the port and to the *waegh* or office of weights (17th century) with an attractive columned gallery and gable. It is now a café-restaurant.

The old orphanage (1630) of Weeshuis contains botanical gardens where exhibitions are held.

Excursions

From Monnickendam you can reach **Marken** and **Volendam** by boat. Boats leave every 30 minutes between 9am and 4:45pm from the Haringburgwal. Information can be obtained at the port or from the VVV Nieuwpoortslaan Loswal, ☎ (029) 95 1998 *(open Apr 1-Oct 1, Mon-Sat 10am-7pm, Oct 1 to Apr 1, Mon-Sat 10am-12:30pm).*

At **Katwoude,** make a point of visiting the **De Jacob Hoeve** cheese farm where you can watch cheese being made according to traditional Dutch recipes. The milk comes from 160 cows, 200 goats and 300 ewes *(admission free).*

You can also visit a clog-maker at Katwoude: **Irene Hoeve,** Hoogedijk 1 *(open daily, admission free).*

Accommodation

▲▲ **Lakeland,** Jachthaven 1, ☎ (029) 95 3751. 110 rooms. Holiday hotel on yacht basin.

▲▲ **Het Wapen van Monnickendam,** Havingstraat 7, ☎ (029) 95 1513.

Food

Nieuw Stuttenburgh, Haringburgwal 2, ☎ (029) 95 1869. Open daily 10am-10pm. Pleasantly located on the yacht basin with fish specialities. R.

De Roef, Noordeinde 40, ☎ (029) 95 1471. Open Tue-Sun noon-9pm. French cuisine in an exceptionally attractive 17th-century building. E.

De Waegh, Haven, ☎ (029) 95 1217. Restaurant on the port, fish specialities. R.

▬ *MARKEN* ★★

13 mi/21 km north-east of Amsterdam. By bus take NZH n° 111 opposite St Nicholas Church in Amsterdam; by car, leave Amsterdam by the S11 and the IJtunnel.

The island of Marken was founded in the 13th century by Frisian monks who farmed the land and raised cattle there.

A windmill, canal and bicycle – a familiar, yet authentic image of Holland.

They built dikes to protect the island from the sea. When the monks left the island in the 14th century, the dikes were neglected; regular floods put an end to agriculture and cattle raising. The residents of Marken turned to fishing. In the beginning, they sailed on North Sea boats or coasting-luggers, but in the 19th and 20th centuries they turned to heavy luggers. They went on to fish in the Zuiderzee using their own boats, known as *botters*. The construction of the Afsluitdijk, closing the Zuiderzee in 1932, put an end to the fishing industry. Today, tourism is Marken's single most important source of revenue.

Linked to the mainland by a dike since the 1930s, the residents have retained their distinctive local customs and a fervent attachment to Protestantism, in spite of the fact that other towns along the coast are Catholic.

The houses of Marken have a distinctive architecture, especially visible around the port area, the Havenbuurt. Perched on their artificial hillocks between the sea and the fields, they are small, adjoining constructions. The houses have a masonry ground floor and a wooden upper floor with an outside staircase. Some are painted green while others are tarred and covered with tiles. Groups of houses are linked by narrow brick roads, and canals are frequently bridged by means of a simple plank.

You'll still see many of Marken's residents dressed in traditional clothing. The women wear full red skirts and short bodices embroidered in a variety of colours or made from pieces of Indonesian batik. Their headgear is very elaborate, consisting of a velvet bonnet worn with a fringe of starched hair. The men wear short close-fitting waistcoats, and trousers full in the thighs and tight at the knees.

After a stroll along the port, turn right toward **Kerkbuurt**, the church district, which is grandly termed 'the capital.' It has remained delightfully traditional. Two small boats are suspended from the vault of the church: a *haringbuis* or herring-fishing boat, and a bark in full sail.

The church *(open May-Oct, Mon-Sat 10am-5pm)* contains model boats made by local residents.

A few yards from the church is the **Marken Museum** *(open Easter-Nov 1, Mon-Sat 10am-4:30pm, Sun noon-4pm)*, which occupies four houses, known as *rookhuisje,* used by fishermen until 1932. You will have no trouble understanding the origin of the name *rookhuisje* (*rook* means smoke and *huisje* house): there is no chimney and smoke goes out directly through a hole in the roof. A number of everyday objects used in Marken are also displayed.

Marken is not totally devoted to the tourist trade. The port has been converted for the use of private boats, but the town is only gradually – and reluctantly – emerging from its age-old isolation.

Parking: Drivers arriving at Marken must leave their cars in the parking lot at the entrance to the village.

In the tourist season you can get from Marken to Volendam by boat (the trip lasts 45 minutes; boats leave Marken and Monnickendam every 30 minutes between 9am and 4:45pm). Information can be obtained at the port.

There are no hotels in this small village, but visitors can stay in nearby Monnickendam or Volendam.

■■■ *VOLENDAM*

13.6 mi/22 km north-east of Amsterdam. By bus, take NSH n° 110 in front of St Nicholas Church in Amsterdam: by road, leave Amsterdam by the S11 and the IJtunnel.

Volendam is the most tourist oriented of the former fishing villages near Amsterdam. Souvenir shops are the centre of the town's economic activity. Volendam's fishermen used to specialize in eels, which flourished in the magnificent breeding grounds of the sea. With the gradual desalination of the water resulting from the closing of the Zuiderzee, the eels became more numerous but also much smaller. There are still a few fishermen and there is even a traditional smokehouse at the port, the **Rokerji.**

Many people in Volendam still wear traditional clothing, which is often superb: full skirts with vertical blue stripes, pleated black skirts, striped aprons and pointed bonnets with the brims curving upward. The men wear baggy black trousers, waist coats, sometimes with silver guilders in place of buttons, and thick round hats. You will be most likely to see them on Sunday mornings outside the church and in the old town centre.

The main road runs along the port on a dike from which you can see the black sails of the fishing boats. It is a typical tourist site, with shops lining both sides of the street. Here you can buy clogs (sometimes made of pottery), beads, pewter and copperware – and even rent a local costume to be photographed in. You will see lots of *Patat Frites* (french fries) restaurants; there are also places where you can sample smoked eel or (from May to September) fresh herring.

De Gouden Kamer (Oude Draaipad 8, *open daily during the summer 9am-6pm*) offers a display of cigar bands. The **Volendam Museum** (Kloosterbuurt 5, *open Easter–mid-Aug, Tues-Sat 10am-noon, 1:30-5pm*), housed in a 19th-century cloister, displays a collection of photos and paintings that give a general idea of Volendam's traditional fishing activities and costumes.

Other places worth visiting include the Fish Market *(open Mon-Fri 10-11am, 4-6pm)*, a pottery-maker (Ventersgracht 1, *open Mon-Fri 8am-5pm)* and a cheese farm, Alide Haeue *(open daily 9am-6pm)*.

You can also get to Marken by boat. Boats leave every 30 minutes. Information is available at the port or at the VVV, Zeestraat 21 *(open Apr-Sept, Mon-Fri 9am-5pm, Sat, Sun 10-5pm, Oct-March, Mon-Fri 11am-4pm)*.

Accommodation

▲▲ **Spaander**, Haven 15, ☎ (029) 936 3595. 100 rooms. Located in an old building on the port.

▲▲ **Th. u. d. Hogen**, Haven 106 on the port, ☎ (029) 936 3775. 14 rooms. Excellent restaurant with fish specialities.

▲▲ **Van Diepen**, Haven 38, ☎ (029) 93 63 705. 40 rooms. On the port with a good restaurant.

Food

There are a dozen restaurants, all on the port, which specialize in fish dishes: for example, **Old Dutch**, **In de Kae**, **We Amvo**.

▬ *EDAM* ★★

18.5 mi/30 km north of Amsterdam. By bus take NSH n° 110 in front of St Nicholas Church, in Amsterdam; by road, leave Amsterdam by the S11 and the IJtunnel.

The town, famous of course for its cheese, also has its own special charm and an aspect that has remained unchanged for centuries.

Edam is one of the best preserved towns on the shores of the Zuiderzee. Its history goes back to the 12th century when peasants and fishermen settled there at the mouth of the Ye or Die. In 1357 a wall, a dike and a port were built, and the town prospered. In the 16th century, more than 33 shipyards were in operation. After the polders were drained, the town became known worldwide for its cheeses – in 1649 it already exported more than 500,000 rounds of cheese. The Office of Weights and Measures on the marketplace recalls that flourishing period. Today the Netherlands produces approximately 176 million pounds/80 million kilos of Edam cheese.

You might include a visit to the cheese market *(open Apr-Sept, Mon-Sun 10am-5pm)*. It was built in 1770 and provides a permanent exhibition on cheese.

To fully appreciate the beauty and prosperity of old Edam, make your way to the **Dam Square**, built on an inland lock dating from 1544. This is the site of the town hall, which was constructed in 1737: there are paintings in the Schepenkamer, or Aldermen's Hall, and a very fine marriage hall with hand-painted wallpaper (information available from the VVV).

On the other side of the Dam you will see the town's oldest stone house (1550), with a magnificent Gothic façade. It remained occupied until 1885. It is now a **museum** *(open Easter-Sept, Mon-Sat 10am-4:30pm, Sun and holidays 2-4:30pm)*.

The museum building dates from the period when the transition between wooden and brick construction was taking place; therefore, it still retains the structure of a wooden house. Its most curious feature is its so-called floating cellar reached from the kitchen-living room. It is a sort of brick box, watertight and lined with tiles, which rises and falls according to the water level. According to legend, it was built by a former sea captain to remind him of a ship's motion at sea. You will also see two seamen's chests with the arms of the town (a bull) and the monogram VOCA *(Verenigde Oostindische Compagnie of Amsterdam)*, and three portraits of notable Edam figures.

To the left of the museum, you can see the tower of the old Church of Our Lady (Speeltoren) dating from 1652. It is now the VVV office *(open Apr-Sept, Mon-Fri 10am-12:30pm 1:30-5pm, Sat noon-5pm; Oct-Mar, Mon-Sat 10:30am-noon)*. Edam's most noteworthy monument however, and the one of which the town is proudest, is the **Grote Kerk,** (Great Church), the St Nicholas Church in flamboyant Gothic style with a magnificent choir screen and stained-glass windows *(open Apr-Oct, daily 2-4:30pm)*.

As originally built in 1475, it was in the form of a cross with a large nave, narrow side aisles and a small choir. In about 1500, the side aisles were enlarged so that the church took the form of a hall. In the early 16th century, the original choir was replaced by the more impressive choir you can see today. After a fire in 1602, the church acquired a new roof and new stained-glass windows, executed at Gouda and remarkably well preserved.

Apart from the impressive interior space, the most striking things about this church are the extraordinary wooden barrel vault and the great organs, originally built by Barend Smit and enlarged in 1716 by M. Verhofstad.

Accommodation

▲▲ **Damhotel,** Keizersgracht 1, ☎ (029) 937 1766. 11 rooms. Located in an attractive old house in the town centre.

▲▲ **De Fortuna,** Spuistraat 1, 3, 5, 7, ☎ (029) 937 1671. 25 rooms. This hotel occupies five 17th-century houses in the heart of town and has a very attractive garden at the water's edge.

Campgrounds

Stanbad, Zeevongareedijk 7a, ☎ (029) 937 1994. 100 sites.

Zuyder-Zee, Zeevongsreedijk 7, ☎ (029) 937 1906. Caters primarily to groups, but 5 individual sites are available.

Windmills provide a picturesque setting for an afternoon fishing expedition.

Food

De Boei, Hoogstraat 8, ☎ (029) 937 1309. Open daily noon-11pm. Traditional soups and fish. R.

Half von Holland, Lingerijde 69, ☎ (029) 937 2546. Open Tues-Sun 11am-9pm. French cuisine. I.

Taveerne We Gevangen Poort, Gevengenpoortsteeg 3, ☎ (029) 937 1971. Open Tues-Sun 11am-8pm. Dutch food served in this restaurant located on the port. I.

▬ *HAARLEM* ★★

12.4 mi/20 km west of Amsterdam (numerous trains from Centraal Station will get you there in 20 minutes). By car, take the A5 to the west.

Located less than half an hour from Amsterdam, Haarlem nevertheless has a charm all its own. There is much to see in the city, from the charming medieval center and the Beguine convent to its art treasures. You'll find the most noteworthy collections in the municipal museum, now known as the **Frans Hals Museum** in honour of the town's most illustrious son, one of the greatest portrait painters of his day.

Haarlem is located on the Spaarne, a river that splits into two arms after Spaarndam, and links the town to the North Sea Canal. Like all small towns in this province near the coast, the area of Haarlem is continually expanding toward the sea. An extensive industrial zone (textile factories, shipyards, pharmaceutical and chemical products, chocolate and flower industries) rings the old town.

Haarlem is mentioned in 10th-century chronicles but it was probably founded somewhat earlier. Lying between two inland seas, Haarlemmermeer and Wijde Vormer, which have now been drained, Haarlem had a precarious existence in its early days. Legend has it that a boy called Peter saved the town from disaster by plugging a hole in the Spaarndam dike to the north-east with his finger, remaining there throughout the night.

It was the first capital of the county of Holland and was fortified toward the middle of the 12th century. The people of Haarlem joined Count William I in the fifth crusade and thereby helped capture the port of Damiette in Egypt in 1219. The small chimes of the Great Church (Grote Kerk) are called *damiettes* to this day in memory of the feat.

In the 14th century a new ring of fortifications was built around the town, which experienced a vigorous growth thanks to trade and, from the 15th century onward, its textile industries. The ramparts have vanished, except for the Amsterdamse Poort with its two pepper-box towers through which, in the terrible winter of 1572-1573, the inhabitants were able to emerge to seek food, taking advantage of the dark night and fog. The town was then engaged in the war of independence and was under siege from the Spaniards. From December 11, 1572, to July 13, 1573, Haarlem's beleaguered inhabitants stubbornly resisted.

The enemy was weakened first by the terrible winter and then by the fumes that rose from the swamps with the return of the warm weather. Nonetheless, Haarlem was forced to surrender and endeavoured to obtain honourable terms by paying a ransom of 240,000 guilders. But the Spanish Duke of Alva wanted revenge for the seven-month siege, which had cost the lives of 10,000 of his soldiers. He was merciless, massacring the 1800 survivors of the Haarlem garrison (which originally numbered 4000) and many of the town's inhabitants.

William of Orange recaptured the city in 1577 and it was incorporated in the united Netherlands. The French Protestants who emigrated there helped in the rebuilding of the old town and in its commercial and cultural development. An era of prosperity began that was to reach its height in the 17th century. This was partly due to the extraordinary passion of the Dutch for tulips. The plant was introduced into the country toward the end of the 16th century by Dutch sailors who regularly landed in Turkish ports. Tulips rapidly became an object of financial speculation, which contributed to the wealth of the Haarlem region. 'Tulipmania' developed in the 17th century, about the year 1636, and eventually reached such a pitch that the value of tulip bulbs rose to fantastic heights. A rare species was worth 4400 guilders and one particular variety, Semper augustus, sold for three times as much. Records of the period refer to tulips that sold for fabulous amounts: flowers became merely a pretext for speculation. The government was obliged to take action, and prices dropped sharply.

Haarlem's decline began one century later, primarily because of English industrial and commercial competition. It persisted until the mid-19th century when the Haarlemmermeer was drained and the resulting polders put under cultivation. The region's economy was further restored by the industrialization of the town and the expansion of flower-cultivation, primarily tulips and hyacinths.

Haarlem's fame as one of the centres of Dutch painting was largely due to the genius of Frans Hals. Yet the reputation of the Haarlem School of Painting had been established 150 years earlier by artists of considerable talent. Historically, the first studio in Haarlem was that of Albert van Ouwater, who is presumed to have been the teacher of Geertgen tot Sint Jans, the greatest Dutch painter of the 15th century. Geertgen was born in Leyden but spent most of his life with the Knights of St John in Haarlem. He created a tradition in art that had a powerful influence on other artists.

Frans Hals (1581-1666) began as an apprentice to Mannerist painter Karel Van Mander and became an artist who had a great influence on younger painters. He is well-known for his portraits. Other artists who studied, or were born, in Haarlem include Jacob van Ruisdael, the great 17th-century landscape painter, and Gerard ter Borch.

Getting to know Haarlem

The city's finest monuments are located around the **Market Place** ★ (Grote Market). The **Great Church** ★★ (Grote Kerk; *open 10am-4pm*) is here, surrounded by small shops whose rents contribute to the church's resources.

Inside the church, 28 pillars support a magnificent 16th-century ribbed vault of cedar wood. Fragments of frescoes are still visible on these pillars. There are several interesting tombstones behind the choir, including those of members of the Shoemakers' Guild and that of poet Willem Bilderdijk (1756-1831).

The organ, built by Christian Müller from 1735 to 1738 and completely restored in 1868, is justifiably famous. It has three keyboards, 68 stops and 5000 pipes, the largest of which is 15.6 in/40 cm in diameter and 33 ft/10 m high. Mozart, Handel and, more recently, Dr. Schweitzer have all played this remarkable instrument.

On the south side of the Market Place you can see a superb example of Dutch Renaissance architecture, the meat market. Constructed in the early 17th century, it is now used for modern art exhibitions *(open Mon-Sat 11am-5pm, Sun*

1-5pm). The town hall ★ is on the west side of the Market Place. At one time the residence of the counts of Holland, this ogival edifice was constructed in the mid-14th century. It remains an extremely interesting building despite many restorations and additions. The large hall on the second floor contains 17th-century chandeliers and stained-glass windows from the Bloemendaal Church (1635-1636).

Return to the meat market, turn right, and Warmoesstraat will bring you to the Frans Hals Museum.

Frans Hals Museum ★★★

Groot Heligland 62, ☎ (023) 31 9180; *open Mon-Sat 11am-5pm, Sun and holidays 1-5pm; f4 admission charge.*

The museum ocupies the Oudemannenhuis, or almshouse, where Frans Hals passed the last years of his life, penniless and abandoned by his many children. The home was founded in 1606. The silent courtyards, the great Renaissance hall, the period furniture and the marble floors combine to create a unique atmosphere for the collection of paintings.

Before reaching the display of Hals's own work, you can see work by other Dutch painters, including *St Luke Painting the Virgin and Child,* by Pieter Pietersz, and *St Christopher and St Mary* by Maerten van Heemskerck. An interesting triptych, *Massacre of the Innocents,* was painted by Cornelis Cornelisz van Haarlem in 1591. The swarming masses of distorted bodies and tortured forms together with the theatrical architecture exemplify Dutch Mannerism.

The eight paintings of the Civic Guards and the Regents are the most noteworthy pieces of Hals's work. You can also trace the evolution of the artist's development through these portraits.

The first painting, *The Banquet of the Corps of Archers of St George* ★★ (1616), is remarkable for its spontaneity achieved through the variety of the officers' stances and expressions. *The Banquet of the Officers of the Company of St Hadrian* ★★ (1627) represents Captain De Wit carving a fowl. The presence of Colonel De Voogt and Lieutenant Akersloot beside him strengthens the balance of the composition. The work is distinguished by the richness of colour in the blue and orange sashes and the red and white flags.

The artist displays his virtuosity in the *Meeting of Officers and Non-Commissioned Officers of the Company of St Hadrian* ★★ (1633). It is evident that a significant development took place in the 17 years between this and the first painting. The officers of 1633 are more mature, more settled and their faces reflect the increased luxury and well-being of Holland. Here, Hals uses a dark rather than a light background, with livelier paint strokes and skillful harmonies.

The *Portrait of Officers of the Corps of Archers of St George* ★ (1639) was the last work produced in this genre. From 1640 on, Hals's work displays a trend toward sobriety and solemnity that dominates the last three portraits of the *Regents.* The first of these, *The Regents of the Company of St Elizabeth* ★★★ (1641), is compact and the sombre hues of the clothes emphasize the facial expressions and gestures.

Frans Hals (1581-1666)

Together with Rembrandt of Amsterdam and Vermeer of Delft, Frans Hals symbolizes Dutch painting, and yet he is little known and little understood.

Frans Hals was born in Antwerp, probably in 1581 (or, as some scholars believe, in 1585). His family was driven for religious reasons to emigrate towards the Protestant North and settle in Haarlem.

Between 1600 and 1603, Frans Hals was apprenticed to the Humanist Mannerist painter Karel van Mander, but it was not until 1610 that he was admitted to the Haarlem Guild of St Luke. His interests were not limited to painting, however. In 1616 he was admitted to the Haarlem Chamber of Rhetoric, which reflects his social standing and his literary tastes.

Hals had ten children from his two marriages, and several of them became artists. He lived and painted his entire life in Haarlem. He is primarily known as a great portraitist. His constant financial difficulties eventually resulted in his being exempted from paying annual dues to the guild and in obtaining a grant of 200 guilders from the town.

As an octogenarian he was admitted to the almshouse and it was undoubtedly in order to pay for his keep there that he painted *The Regents* in 1664, one of his best-known works.

The Regents of the Almshouse ★★★ painted 23 years later (1664) is more aggressive, even a trifle cynical, with a Regent who is obviously drunk. In the same year, another painting, *The Regents of the Almshouse* ★★★, further underlines the cold and forbidding characters of the Regents. Their bony countenances and bleak expressions suggest souls of granite. Frans Hals displays an astonishing sobriety in these two pictures: elimination of colour, simplified composition and a lack of detail. The work of an artist who may be considered one of the greatest portrait-painters of the Dutch school reflects a truly astonishing development.

A new wing contains a collection of modern and contemporary art comprising paintings, engravings, sculpture, objets d'art and ceramics. In addition to work by artists from Haarlem and its environs there are works by Dutch Impressionists and Expressionists, the COBRA group and such contemporaries as Isaac Israels, Herman Kruyder, Jan Sluyters and Karel Appel.

Around Frans Hals's House

Leaving the museum, take the Groot Heiligland to the Great Church and, on the choir side, walk along the Damstraat until you reach the Spaarne. On the corner is the old Office of Weights and Measures, the Waag ★, which was built in 1598 and is now a café.

Follow the river to your left until you reach the Teyler Museum, located at n° 16 *(open Oct-Feb Mon-Sat 10am-5pm, Sun 1-5pm)*. This was the first museum in the Netherlands and occupies an 18th-century townhouse. It was founded in 1778 by Pieter Teyler who specified in his will that a substantial part of his fortune should be devoted to the creation of a museum of the arts and sciences. It contains palaeontological and mineralogical collections and scientific apparatus (for studying physics and chemistry) but it is especially noteworthy for its drawings and paintings. In the section devoted to physics and chemistry materials (rooms 3 and 4), you will see the model of an electrical machine invented by Martinus van Marum (circa 1750-1837), a doctor who became professor of physics at Haarlem University.

The collections of drawings, engravings and etchings are exhibited on a temporary basis in room 5. They include drawings of the Dutch, Italian and French schools — in particular, work by Rembrandt, Ruisdael, Michelangelo, Raphael, Claude Lorrain, François Boucher and Watteau — together with engravings and etchings by Rembrandt, Goltzius and Lucas van Leyden. Permission to see the portfolios (on Tuesday and Friday afternoons) of those drawings not on display can be obtained on written application to the curator.

Room 6 is set aside for temporary exhibitions while room 7 houses paintings by 19th-century Dutch artists. The numismatic room is open on the first Tuesday of the month during the museum hours.

Cross the bridge over the Spaarne, and turn left on Spaarnwouderstraat, which leads to the Amsterdam Gate (Amsterdamse Poort), built in the late 14th century. Although the part facing the town was restored in the early 18th century, the gate has retained its medieval aspect with its pepper-box towers and massive quadrangular dungeon.

Continue on the same street beyond the Amsterdam Gate, and turn to the left on Papentorenvest, cross the Spaarne again and left at the end of the bridge. Take the first street on the right to the **Teyler's Almshouse ★**, a Beguine convent built in 1787 with an inner courtyard surrounded by 24 small houses.

Return to the quay bordering the Spaarne, turn left and then left again after the bridge onto Nieuwegracht. Jansstraat, the first street on the left, will bring you back to the Grote Markt. You will pass by the **Walloon Church ★**, Haarlem's oldest church, which is located in a very attractive district with several small houses and Beguine almshouses. The church is in fact a former Beguine Chapel and dates from the 16th century. If you should be there on a Sunday morning (10:30am-noon) don't be surprised to hear the liturgy in French: this tradition was inherited from the French Huguenot refugees.

Around the church are numerous small shops: antiques dealers, bookstores and craft shops selling musical instruments and jewelry. Haarlem also has a number of elegant shops, department stores, restaurants and cafés grouped in the area reserved for pedestrians.

Accommodation

▲▲▲ **The Golden Tulip Lion d'Or**, Kruisweg 34-36, ☎ (023) 32 1750. 36 rooms. Conveniently located near the station, with a good restaurant.

▲▲ **Waldor**, Jansweg 40, ☎ (023) 31 2622. 20 rooms. Close to the town centre in a beautiful house.

▲ **Die Raeckse,** Raaks 1-3, ☎ (023) 32 6629. 30 rooms. Located in the centre of the town, in an old house.

▲ **Carillon,** Grote Markt 27, ☎ (023) 31 0591. 34 rooms. Centrally located, with a French restaurant.

▲ **Zijlhoeve,** Zijlweg 159-161, ☎ (023) 32 5909. 18 rooms. Located within minutes of the town centre.

Food

De Vergulde Arend, Grote Markt 10, ☎ (023) 32 4530. Open daily 10am-10pm. Traditional Dutch cuisine; a few rooms are also available. R.

On the Grote Markt you will also find:

La Brochette, Grote Markt 23, ☎ (023) 31 7786. Open daily noon-10pm. This restaurant serves both French and Dutch food. R.

Le Carillon, Grote Markt 27, ☎ (023) 31 0591. This small French restaurant is located in an attractive old house. R.

The Coach House Inn, Ged Oude Gracht 34, ☎ (023) 31 2760. Good Dutch food at reasonable prices. R.

Alfonso's Café Cantina, Oude Groenmarkt 8, ☎ (023) 31 7434. Mexican food. I.

The Golden Tulip Lion d'Or and **Die Raeckse** hotels also have excellent restaurants.

Useful address

VVV, in front of the station, ☎ (023) 31 9059. *Open Mon-Sat 10am-5pm.*

▬ *MUIDEN CASTLE*★ (Muiderslot)

Herengracht 1, 9.9 mi/16 km east of Amsterdam. Take buses n° 136 or n° 138 from Amstelstation, II, E5. By car, take the E8 in the direction of Amersfoort. *Guided tours only Apr-Sept, Mon-Fri 10am-5pm, Sun and holidays 1-5pm, Oct-Mar, Mon-Fri 10am-4pm, Sun and holidays 1-4pm; f4 admission charge.*

Muiderslot was built in 1205 by the Bishop of Utrecht. This impressive brick fortress with its powerful circular towers has been converted into an historical museum. It houses a collection of furniture from the first half of the 17th century, weapons, armour and tapestries. One of the tapestries (Flanders, 15th century) depicts the meeting between Alexander the Great and the mother, wife and daughters of Darius III Codomannus, defeated in 333 BC by the Macedonian conqueror at the Battle of Issus.

Accommodation

▲▲ **Nooitgedacht,** Dorpstraat 29, ☎ (029) 42 1303. 6 rooms. There is a restaurant and café.

Food

De Doelen, Sluis 1. Fish specialities.

Graaf Floris V van Muiden, Herengracht 72. Attractive decor, Dutch cuisine.

Comenius (1592-1670)

Born in Moravia in what is now Czechoslovakia, Comenius studied at Nassau in Germany, then returned to his native land where he was ordained a priest in the church of the Moravian Brethren.

This sect was an offshoot of the reformist movement of the Hussites (16th century) or, more precisely, of the most radical group, the Taborites. To escape from the persecution of Czech Protestants by the Hapsburg Ferdinand II, Comenius emigrated to Poland in 1628 and then to Holland in 1656. Comenius is known not so much for his philosophy (he wrote the *Pansophia* but never published it) as he is for his *Didacta magna*, a work on education and teaching methods of such originality that it is regarded as the forerunner of modern pedagogy.

▬ *NAARDEN* ★

14.8 mi/24 km east of Amsterdam. Take buses 136, 137 or 138 from Amstelstation, II, E5 (stopover in Muiden). By car, take the E8 in the direction of Amersfoort. This town of 17,300 inhabitants was founded circa 1350, conquered by the Spaniards in 1572 and, in the 17th century, was Amsterdam's first line of defense against invasion from the east. It has a powerful star-shaped citadel designed by Adriaan Dortsman (completed in 1685), which was formerly surrounded by swamps and wide ditches.

Following the road from Amsterdam, you will come to the Gothic Great Church (Grote Kerk) built between 1380 and 1440. On Good Friday every year, a performance of Johann Sebastian Bach's *St. Matthew Passion* attracts a large number of music enthusiasts (reservations: 98 Juliana van Stolberglaan, ☎ (021) 17 329).

Leaving the church to your left, you will come to the **town hall** *(stadhuis)*, a fine building in the Dutch Renaissance style. Exhibitions are held here in the summer months.

Marktstraat, opposite the town hall on the right, will bring you to the ramparts. On a small square to your left notice a sculpture (1969) by Ek van Zanten. On the left is a statue of Czech humanist Jan Amos Komensky, commonly known as Comenius, by Vincent Makovsky (1957). Return to the interior of the citadel by the Utrecht Gate (1682). After the gate, turn to the right and cross the base of the Orange Bastion. Continue along Gansoordstraat where, at n° 52, you will see a 17th-century residence followed by several 18th-century houses.

At the end of this street, turn left on Klosterstraat. A barracks is installed in an old convent on your right. The chapel was dedicated in the 17th century to the Walloon Church. Comenius, who fled to Holland in 1656, is buried here.

Nearby (1.2 mi/2 km from the fortress of Naarden) is the huge recreation park and port of **Naarderbos**, located on the edge of the Gooimeer. Here you can enjoy strolling or bicycling, and there are stretches of beach for swimming, fishing or sailing.

Amsterdam's Centraal Station, the hub of the city's transportation system.

Accommodation

▲▲ **De Beurs,** Markstraat 66, ☎ (021) 594 4868. 7 rooms. Centrally located in a pleasant old house.

▲ **Huize Jaäl,** Huizerstraatweg 107, ☎ (021) 594 5228.

Food

De Gooische Brasserie, Cattenhagestraat 9, ☎ (021) 594 8803. Open daily. Dutch and French cuisine with beautiful terrace overlooking the church. R.

De Kapschuur, Kerkepad 1, ☎ (021) 594 1957. Closed Mon. Known for its pancakes. I.

De Poorter van Naarden, Ruysdaelplein 35, ☎ (021) 594 6007. Closed Tues. Very attractive café, wine by the glass and home-made snacks. R.

Theehuis Bos en Hei, Oud Huizerweg 30. Tearooms. R.

AMSTERDAM ADDRESSES

This section includes a list of hotels and restaurants (classified according to type of cuisine), cafés, nightclubs, plus a list of the best shops, classified by the items they sell.

SYMBOLS USED

Hotels

The hotels fall into several categories, and the prices quoted reflect the cost of a double room. Rates may vary within a given category according to the amenities offered, i.e., location, view, terrace, etc. The prices generally include breakfast. Prices should be viewed as approximate indications only; you should request the exact amount when reserving.

▲▲▲▲ Luxury hotel, over f250
▲▲▲ First-class hotel, f180-f250
▲▲ Moderate hotel, f100-f180
▲ Inexpensive hotel, f75-f100.

Restaurants

The restaurants are classified according to the type of cuisine. The Dutch tend to eat dinner early and most restaurants open at 6pm. Don't wait too late to eat; many restaurants close at 10 or 11pm.

The prices for restaurants are classified in three categories:
E Expensive
R Reasonable
I Inexpensive

CONTENTS

Hotels 117
Restaurants 120
Cafés 122
Proeflokaal 123
Nightlife.. 123
Shopping... 125
Art galleries.................................... 127

HOTELS

Among the many hotels in Amsterdam we have made a point of singling out those with some special feature to recommend them.

▲▲▲▲ **Grand Hotel Krasnapolsky**, Dam 9, I, B4, ☎ 554 6048. 370 rooms. Located in the medieval town, this historic hotel founded more than a century ago began as a simple café. It has several restaurants (including a Japanese one) and a garage – a rare feature in Amsterdam.

▲▲▲▲ **Hotel Pulitzer**, Prinsengracht 315-331, I, C2, ☎ 22 8333. 240 rooms. Arranged very tastefully, this modern hotel is in a former warehouse. Located near the art galleries and the Jordaan.

▲▲▲ **Ambassade**, Herengracht 341, I, C3, ☎ 26 2333. 42 rooms. Well-located not far from the historic heart of the city, and tastefully housed in a building from the Golden Age.

▲▲▲ **Arthur Frommer**, Noorderstraat 46, I, E4, ☎ 22 0328. 90 rooms. An old residence near the Prinsengracht and close to the major museums.

▲▲▲ **Atlas**, Van Eeghenstraat 64, I, F1, ☎ 76 6336. 24 rooms. In a villa on the edge of the Vondelpark near the museums.

▲▲▲ **Estherea**, Singel 303-309, I, C3, ☎ 24 5146. 75 rooms. Near the flower market, in a very old renovated building with typical Dutch atmosphere.

▲▲▲ **Euromotel**, Joan Muyskenweg 10, II, F5, ☎ 65 8181. 128 rooms. In south Amsterdam at the entrance to the city. Parking is available; tram n° 25 stops just opposite and will get you to the city and Centraal Station in a few minutes.

▲▲▲ **Jan Luyken**, Jan Luykenstraat 58, I, F2, ☎ 76 4111. 63 rooms. A former villa, this attractive hotel is conveniently located near the major museums.

▲▲▲ **Museum**, P.C. Hooftstraat 2, I, E2, ☎ 62 1402. 116 rooms. Recently modernized, not far from the Rijksmuseum. Parking available nearby.

▲▲▲ **Trianon**, J.W. Brouwerstraat 3, II, D3, ☎ 73 2073. 52 rooms. Almost part of the Concertgebouw and not far from the museums.

▲▲ **Agora**, Singel 462, I, D3, ☎ 27 2200. 13 rooms. An old building very pleasantly modernized near the flower market. Breakfast is served in the garden in summer.

▲▲ **Canal House**, Keizersgracht 148, I, A3, ☎ 22 5182. 27 rooms. Not far from the Dam in a 17th-century building filled with antiques. A large dining room opens onto a garden.

▲▲ **Cok**, Koninginneweg 34-36, II, D2, ☎ 64 6111. 68 rooms. Near the Vondelpark. Very convenient for families: many of the rooms have kitchenettes, and washing machines are available to guests.

▲▲ **De Gouden Kettingh**, Keizersgracht 268, I, C3, ☎ 24 8287. 18 rooms. This family-run hotel is not far from the Dam.

▲▲ **Marianne**, Nicolas Maesstraat 107, II, D2, ☎ 79 7972. 15 rooms. In south Amsterdam near the Vondelpark. Pleasant atmosphere.

▲▲ **Mikado**, Amstel 107-111, I, D5, ☎ 23 7068. 26 rooms. In a particularly attractive district near the Blauw Brug.

▲▲ **Rokin**, Rokin 73, I, C4, ☎ 26 7456. 38 rooms. Not far from The House of the Three Canals.

The tower of the Westerkerk rises above the houseboats on the Prinsegracht.

▲ **Belga,** Hartenstraat 8, I, B3, ☎ 24 9080. 10 rooms. In a small street not far from the Dam, this is a small, quiet and attractive hotel.

▲ **Museumzicht,** Jan Luykenstraat 22, I, F2, ☎ 71 2954. 14 rooms. This hotel is on a quiet street very close to the museums.

▲ **Van Haalen,** Prinsengracht 520, I, E4, ☎ 26 4334. 17 rooms. Located in the centre on the canals.

▲ **Van Onna,** Bloemgracht 102, I, B2, ☎ 26 5801. 9 rooms. Located in the picturesque district of Amsterdam, the Jordaan.

▲ **Wijnnobel,** Vossiusstraat 9, I, E2, ☎ 62 2298. 12 rooms. On the edge of the Vondelpark, this attractive house is filled with antiques.

Youth hostels

Hostels offer the cheapest accommodation. Prices range from f15 for a single to up to f90 for a double room. Breakfast is not usually provided in hostels. Some have a curfew, but it is generally quite late (after midnight).

Cok Student Class, Koningslaan 1, II, D2, ☎ 664 6111. 60 rooms. This hostel is well located opposite lovely Vondelpark.

Kabul, Warmoestraat 38-42, I, B4, ☎ 23 7158. 58 rooms. This is very conveniently located, within easy walking distance of Centraal Station. No curfew.

Vondel Park, Zandpad 5, I, E2, ☎ 83 1744. 40 rooms. An official Dutch youth hostel located near Vondelpark, it has a restaurant and café.

Campgrounds

There are several campgrounds easily accessible from the city centre. The rates range from f25 to f40 per night for a site. It is advisable to reserve in advance, especially during summer months.

Amsterdam Bos, Kleine Noorddijk 1, Aalsmeer, ☎ 41 6868. 350 sites. This area is quite a distance from the centre but can be reached by taking bus n° 171 or 172. Open Apr-Oct.

Amsterdamsche IJsclub, IJsbaanpad 45, ☎ 62 0916. 550 sites. This is just 10 minutes by tram from the centre (take n° 16 or 24). It has a shop and restaurant. Open Mar-Oct.

Gaasper Camping, Loosdrechtdreef 7, ☎ 96 7326. 300 sites. The campground is 20 minutes from the centre and is well-equipped for families, with playgrounds, etc. Open all year.

■■■ *RESTAURANTS*

Dutch

Bols Taverne, Rozengracht 106, I. B5, ☎ 24 5752. Closed Sun, Mon. This restaurant specializes in fish dishes, and you will find generous portions and good service here. R.

Dikker en Thijs, Leidsestraat 82, I. D3, ☎ 26 7721. Closed Sun. This is one of Amsterdam's best restaurants. E.

Dorrius, N.Z. Voorburgwal 336-342, I. C3, ☎ 23 5245. Open daily. Traditional specialities here. R.

De Gouden Reael, Zandhoek 14, II. A4, ☎ 23 3883. Closed Sun. Tasty meat and fish dishes in an intimate atmosphere with a view of the harbour. E.

De Kelderhof, Prinsengracht 494, I. D2-3, ☎ 22 0682. Open daily. Very attractive decor and covered terrace.

Oesterbar, Leidseplein 10, I. D2, ☎ 26 3463. Open daily. Pleasant closed-in terrace where you can eat delicious oysters and fish specialities. E.

De Port Van Cleve, N.Z. Voorburgwal 178-180, I. C3, ☎ 24 0047. Open daily. This traditional restaurant offers a children's menu. R.

t'Seepaerd, Rembrandtsplein 22, I. A4, ☎ 22 1759. Closed Sun. Fish specialities. R.

De Trachter, Hobbemakade 63, I. F3, ☎ 71 2263. Closed Sun. Great traditional dishes and nouvelle Dutch cuisine at reasonable prices. R.

D'Vijff Vlieghen, Spuistraat 294-302, I. C3, ☎ 24 8369. Open daily. Located in a charming old building, this is one of the most renowned Dutch restaurants in the city. E.

French

De Gelaarsde Kat, Oude Hoogstraat 20, I. C4-5, ☎ 23 1947. Open daily. Well-prepared French cuisine. R.

De Kikker, Egelantierstraat 128-130, I. AB2, ☎ 27 9198. Open daily. Haute cuisine in this attractive café-theatre-style restaurant in the Jordaan. R.

Les Quatre Canetons, Prinsengracht 1111, I. E5, ☎ 24 6307. Closed Sun. Nouvelle cuisine, an excellent wine list and fish specialities in a lovely decor. E.

La Rive, Prof. Tulpplein 1, I. EF6, ☎ 22 6060. Open daily. An intimate atmosphere welcomes you to this most fashionable restaurant in the Amstel Hotel. Jacket and tie required. E.

De Smoeshaan, Leisekade 9 P, I, D2, ☎ 25 0368. Dinner only. Located near the Opera and theatres, this restaurant is frequented by artists and actors. There is a restaurant on the first floor and a more reasonably priced café, with food, in the basement. R-E.

Valentijn, Kloveniersburgwal 6-8, I, B5, ☎ 24 2028. Closed Mon, Tues. Located near the Nieuwmarkt, specializing in nouvelle cuisine. E.

Warstein, Spuistraat 266-268, I, C3, ☎ 22 9609. You can select from among several reasonably priced menus in a particularly attractive setting. R.

Indian

The Guru of India, Lange Leidsedwarsstraat 56, I, D2, ☎ 24 6966. Open daily. This small restaurant serves delicious Indian food. R.

The Tandoor, Leidseplein 19, I, D2, ☎ 23 4415. Open daily. Amsterdam's finest Indian restaurant. E.

Indonesian

Bali, Leidsestraat 95, I, D3, ☎ 22 7878. Open daily. Excellent food in this conveniently located restaurant. R.

Culibang, Runstraat 10, I, C2, ☎ 26 9755. Dinner only; closed Mon. This small, popular restaurant is a good place to try an Indonesian *rijsttafel* (rice table). I.

Jayakarta, Rembrandtsplein 16, I, D4, ☎ 25 5569. Open daily. A good place to try after a visit to Rembrandt's house. R.

Sama Sebo, P.C. Hoofstraat 27, I, E2, ☎ 72 8146. Open daily. This is one of the city's best Indonesian restaurants. It is wise to reserve in advance. R.

Special, Nieuwe Leliestraat 142, I, B2, ☎ 24 9706. Open daily. Located in the Jordaan area, it serves excellent specialities in an authentic decor. R.

Tempo Doeloe, Utrechtsestraat 75, I, E5, ☎ 25 6718. Open daily. Delicious *rijsttafel,* but watch out: when a dish is marked 'hot,' it is generally very hot! E.

Chinese

Dynasty, Reguliersdwarsstraat 30, I, D4, ☎ 26 8400. Dinner only; closed Tues. An exotic decor and delicious food make this one of Amsterdam's best Chinese restaurants. There is a garden for summer dining. Reserve in advance. E.

Treasure, N.Z. Voorburgwal 115, I, C3, ☎ 23 4061. Open daily. You will find a very large selection here, but if in doubt, try the *dim sum* (dumplings stuffed with a wide selection of fillings). I.

Italian

Casa di David, Singel 426, I, D3, ☎ 24 5093. You'll get good value for your money here. I.

Tartufo, Singel 449, I, D3, ☎ 27 7175. Closed Sat, Sun lunch. Delicious pasta downstairs, a more complete (and expensive) menu upstairs. R-E.

Japanese

Kyo, Jan Luykenstraat 2 a, I, E2, ☎ 71 6916. Closed Sun. Excellent food in a decor of rice paper screens and mats. R.

Yamazoto (Okura Hotel), Ferdinand Bolstraat 333, II, D4, ☎ 78 7111. Open daily. Here you will find traditional cuisine, including sashimi and tempura dishes. E.

Mexican

Caramba, Lindengracht 342, I, A3, ☎ 27 1188. Open daily. This is a pleasant place for a meal after a stroll in the Jordaan. R.

Rose's Cantina, Reguliersdwarsstraat 38, I, D3, ☎ 25 9797. Open daily. This is a very popular restaurant these days. You can enjoy an American cocktail at the bar while waiting for a table. R.

▬ *CAFÉS*

For a description of Amsterdam's unique brown cafés, see p. 26.

De Blincker, St Barberenstraat 7, I, C4, ☎ 23 5723. Open 10-1am. Close to Mes Street where there are several theatres.

Café Américain, Leidseplein 24-28, I, D2, ☎ 24 5322. Open 11-2am. This large Art-Deco-style café is located in the Hotel Américain.

De Engelbewaardor, Klovenieisburgwal 59, I, C4, ☎ 25 3772. Brown café frequented by students and artists.

Gollem, Raamsteeg 4, I, B2, ☎ 26 6645. Located between the Spuistraat and the Singel, this crowded and lively café is a beer lover's paradise with 200 varieties of beer from around the world.

Hoppe, Spui 18-20, I, C3, ☎ 24 0756. Open 10-1am. Renowned brown café dating from the 17th century. A favourite with Amsterdammers, the Hoppe is always full.

De Koophandel, Blaemgracht 49, I, B2, ☎ 24 9741. Open to 3am. Located in the Jordaan, this is a pleasant place to linger over a beer.

Oblomov, Reguliersdwarsstraat 40, I, D4, ☎ 24 1074. Open 10-1am. Art-Déco design, popular with artists and intellectuals.

De Reiger, Nieuwe Leliestraat 34, I, B2, ☎ 24 7426. Open 10-1am. Brown café in the Jordaan where you can have a simple meal. Popular with students and artists who live and work in the neighbourhood.

Schiller Café, Rembrandtsplein 26-36, I, D4, ☎ 23 1660. Open 4pm-1am. Art-Deco style, with an intimate atmosphere. A meeting place for Amsterdam's intellectuals.

Van Puffelen, Prinsengracht 377, I, C2. A noisy and crowded café; outdoor tables are placed on a barge on the canal during warm weather.

Walem, Keisersgracht 449, I, D3, ☎ 25 3544. Open 10-1am. One terrace facing the canal, another in the garden. A popular place for artists.

Wet Paleis, Paleisstraat 16, I, B4, ☎ 26 0600. Open 10-1am. Favoured by students from the art school, artists and painters. Good food. Located just behind the Royal Palace (Dam).

Wildschut, Roelof Hartplein 1, II, D3, ☎ 73 8622. Open 10-1am. Art-Deco style, frequented by journalists.

The elegant façade of a fashionable Amsterdam café.

PROEFLOKAALS

This is an institution in Amsterdam, the word literally meaning testing place. The *proeflokaal* is always crammed with barrels, bottles, earthenware jugs and curios, and you taste your wines and spirits in a friendly, 'brown' atmosphere. Customers come here to chat over their drinks. The smell of beer, wine and liquor mixes with the smoke to create a unique ambience.

The· oldest are:

De Drie Flesches, Gravenstraat 18, behind the Nieuwekerk, I, B4, ☎ 24 8443. A superb 17th-century interior.

Wijnand Fockink, Pijlsteeg 31, I, B4, ☎ 24 3989. Here the liquor is as old as the setting itself and bears such curious names as *Hemdje licht op*, literally meaning take off your shirt, *Juffertje in het groen*, young girl in green, or *Naveltje bloot*, which means bare navel!

You will also find plenty to enjoy at **Hooghoudt**, Reguliersgracht 11, I, D4, ☎ 25 5030, and at the **Admiraal**, Herengracht 319, I, C3, ☎ 25 4334.

NIGHTLIFE

Classical music, opera, dance and theatre

Art Theater, Kerkstraat 4, I, D3, ☎ 25 9495. English-language theatre performances.

Concertgebouw, Van Baerlestraat 98, II, F4, ☎ 71 8345. Amsterdam's world-renowned orchestra gives concerts here.

De Nieuwe Kerk, Dam I, B4, ☎ 26 8168. Organ concerts.

Het Muziektheater, Waterlooplein 22, I, D5, ☎ 25 5455. The new theatre on Waterlooplein showcases Dutch and international opera and dance troupes.

Stadsschouwburg, Leidseplein 26, I, D2, ☎ 24 2311. Opera, theatre and dance performances.

Theater Carré, Amstel 115, I, D4, ☎ 22 5225. Originally built as a circus in 1887, the theatre now presents concerts, ballets and modern dance performances, and plays as well as international circus troupes.

Live jazz, blues and rock

Bamboo Bar, Lange Leidsedwarsstraat, I, D2, ☎ 24 3993. Jazz and blues in tropical setting.

Bimhuis, Oude Schans 73-77, I, C5, ☎ 23 3373. Run by the Jazz Musicians Association, mainly modern jazz concerts are held Thursday to Saturday, with improvisational sessions Monday to Wednesday.

Café Alto, Korte Leidsedwarsstraat 115, I, D2, ☎ 26 3249. Jazz in small café near the Leidseplein.

Joseph Lamm Jazz Club, Van Diemenstraat 8, II, A4, ☎ 22 8086. Large popular jazz club in north Amsterdam.

De Kroeg, Lijnbaansgracht 163, I, C2, ☎ 25 0177. Jazz and salsa music in this Jordaan nightclub.

Maloe Melo, Lijnbaansgracht 160, I, C2, ☎ 25 3300. Famous as the 'home of the blues', a great place for blues enthusiasts.

De Stip, Lijnbaansgracht 161, I, C2, ☎ 27 9692. Rock, jazz, blues and reggae concerts every night except Sunday.

Discotheques

Boston Club, Kattengat 1, I, A4, ☎ 24 5561. The Sonesta Hotel's sophisticated club.

Juliana's, Apollolaan 138, II, E3, ☎ 73 7313. The Hilton Hotel's nightclub and discotheque.

Mazzo, Rozengracht 114, I, B2, ☎ 26 7500. Originally a club for audio-visual artists, it has become a favourite of musicians, artists, intellectuals and students for dancing or simply watching the video presentation.

Zorba the Buddha, Oudezijds Voorburgwal 216, I, B4, ☎ 25 9642. Run by the disciples of the Indian guru Bhagwan, a varied clientele is attracted by its ultra-modern decor and lively dance music.

Cultural centres

De Meervaart, Osdorpplein 205, ☎ 10 7393. On the outskirts of town (take tram 1, or bus 19 or 23, to Osdorpplein), it hosts theatre and dance performances, concerts (classical, rock, jazz and blues) and film screenings. A blues festival is held here in the spring.

Melkweg, Lijnbaansgracht 234, I, D2, ☎ 24 1777. In the 60s and 70s this was the counter-culture's favourite meeting place, with its rock concerts, poetry sessions, bookstore and stalls where you could buy Oriental clothing, incense, herbs and marijuana. The atmosphere has changed somewhat, though it has remained popular. There are theatre and dance performances, concerts, a dance hall, cinema, and restaurant.

Odeon, Singel 460, I, D3, ☎ 24 9711. An old theatre restored to house a bar, theatre, dance floor (mostly music of the 60s), and jazz performances.

Shaffy, Keizersgracht 324, I, C3, ☎ 26 2321. A cultural centre where you can enjoy theatre, cinema and concerts. The café and restaurant are frequented by artists.

■■ SHOPPING

Shopping districts

P.C. Hooftstraat, I, E2. This is the most fashionable shopping street in Amsterdam, with particularly elegant boutiques such as Focke & Melzer, where you can buy attractive chinaware and crystal.

The Jordaan, I, AB2. There are a number of attractive clothing shops and book stores, jewelers and decorative art shops.

Kalverstraat and Nieuwendijk, I, BC4. Some 250,000 visitors frequent this pedestrian area each week. Here you will find dress shops, jewelers, record shops and a large number of small restaurants and snack bars.

Department stores

De Bijenkorf, Damark 90, I, B4, ☎ 21 8080. This is the largest and best known of Amsterdam's department stores. It is also the most fashionable and most expensive.

Hema is a department store with branches all over town, including: Ferdinand Bolstraat 93, II, D4, ☎ 76 3223; Kinterstraat 126, II, C2, ☎ 83 4511; and Reguliersbreestraat, I, D4, ☎ 24 6506. It is definitely Amsterdam's cheapest and is the place to go for food and household items.

Vroom & Dreesman (V & D), Kalverstraat 201, I, C4, ☎ 22 0171; Bilderdijkstraat 37, I, C1, ☎ 18 0104. Prices here are lower than at De Bijenkorf's, but the goods are less elegant.

Markets

Antiques, Antiekmarkt De Looier, Elandsgracht 109, I, C2, Thurs-Sat 11am-5pm. In summer you can also find antiques at **Nieuwmarkt,** I, B5, Sun 10am-5pm.

Book market, Oudemanhuispoort, I, C4. Opposite the entrance to the university. Old books at very reasonable prices. Mon-Sat 10am-4pm.

Flea market, Waterlooplein, I, C5. This is Amsterdam's oldest market. Mon-Sat 10am-4pm. Hundreds of stalls sell everything from clothing and household items to old prints, woodcuts and magazine illustrations.

Flower market, Singel, I, D4. Mon-Sat 9am-5pm. Besides an extraordinary variety of fresh flowers, you will find bulbs and beautiful arrangements of dried flowers.

General market, Albert Cuypstraat, II, D4, is Amsterdam's best-known market, with food products from all over the world, clothing, shoes and plants.

Noordermarkt, I, A3, is a small flea market (especially for furniture and clothes). Open Mon morning.

Stamp market, Nieuwezijds Voorburgwal, I, C3. Open Wed and Sat 1-4pm.

Auction houses

P. Brandt, Keizersgracht 738, I, D5, ☎ 24 8662.
Christie's, Corn. Schuytstraat 57, II, D3, ☎ 64 2011.
Gijselman & Zn, Singel, 118, I, A4, ☎ 23 3558.
Sotheby's, Rokin 102, I, C4, ☎ 27 5656.

Van Gendt Book Auctions, Keizersgracht 96, I, A3, ☎ 23 4107.

De Zwaan, Keizersgracht 474, I, D3, ☎ 22 0447.

Shops

Antiques

Frides Lameris, Nieuwe Spiegelstraat 55, I, D3, ☎ 26 4066.

Do Looier, Elandsgracht 109, I, C2, ☎ 24 9038.

't Portaal, Vijzelstraat 101, I, D4, ☎ 26 6147.

M.L. Woltering, Nieuwe Spiegelstraat 53, I, D3, ☎ 22 2240.

Books

Allert de Lange, Damrak 62, I, B4, ☎ 24 6744. Wide range of foreign books.

Athenaeum, Spui 14-16, I, C3, ☎ 24 2972. This is a good place to find international magazines and newpapers.

Kok, Oude Hoogstraat 14-18, I, C4, ☎ 23 1191. Old books.

Slegte, Kalverstraat 48-52, I, C4, ☎ 22 5933. Secondhand books.

Cigars

P.J.C. Hajenius, Rokin 92-96, I, C4, ☎ 23 7494. The best-known of Amsterdam's cigar stores.

Clothes

Edgar's Boutique, Beethovenstraat 52, II, E3, ☎ 62 7460. Original styles by Edgar Vos and other Dutch designers.

Frank Govers, Keizergracht 500, I, D3, ☎ 22 8670. Haute couture.

John & Vera Hartman, Prinsengracht 176, I, B2. Contemporary clothing.

Liesbeth Rouyaards, Prinsengracht 6, I, A3, ☎ 26 5026. Avant-garde Dutch designer.

Max Heymans, Nicolaas Witsenstraat 16, II, E3. Elegant and expensive clothes.

Peter Rozemeyer, Singel 406, I, A4. Unique Dutch designer clothes.

Reflections, P.C. Hooftstraat 66, I, E2, ☎ 664 0040. Designer clothes.

Crafts

Binnenhuis, Huidenstraat 3, I, C3, 22 1584. Contemporary Dutch designs.

Metz & Co, Keizersgracht 455, I, D3, ☎ 24 8810. China, fabrics and furniture.

Rivet, Elandsgracht 69, I, C2, ☎ 23 6923. Leather bags and suitcases.

't Spinnewiel, St Antoniebreestraat 32, I, C5. Ceramics.

Wouters, Ferdinand Bolstraat 113, I, F4, ☎ 662 8784. Interior decoration.

Food and wine

Dikker & Thijs, Leidsestraat 82, I, D3, ☎ 26 7721. Delicatessen.

Fedduzzi Gastronomie, Nieuwe Weteringstraat 17, I, E3, ☎ 25 9562. Cheeses.

Keyzer, Prinsengracht 180, I, B3, ☎ 24 0823. Coffee and tea.
Paul Année, Runstraat 25, I, C2, ☎ 23 5322. Excellent pastry and bread shop.
Warmolts Wijn, Maasstraat 72, II, E4, ☎ 662 0448. Cheeses and wines.

Jewelry, diamonds

Amsterdam Diamond Center, Rokin, 1-15, I, B4, ☎ 24 5787.
Coster Diamonds, Paulus Potterstraat 2-4, I, E3, ☎ 76 2222.
Schaap en Citroen, Kalverstraat 1, I, C4, ☎ 26 6691. Original silver jewelry.
Siebel Juweliers, Kalverstraat 121, I, C4, ☎ 23 8590. Jewelry.
Van Moppes, Albert Cuypstraat 2-6, II, D4, ☎ 76 1242. Diamonds.

Unusual boutiques

E. Kramer Poppendokter, Reestraat 18-20, I, B2-3, ☎ 26 5274. Antique dolls.
Glass in Lood Atelier, Egelantierstraat 19, I, A2, Light fixtures and glass objects, many in Art-Deco style.
Het Teinenhuis, Bilderdijkstraat 94, I, C1, ☎ 18 1255. An enormous collection of train models and accessories.
Posthumus, Sint Luciensteeg 225, I, B3, ☎ 38 1382. A wide choice of personalized stationery.
Raining Cats and Dogs, Reestraat 24, I, B2-3, ☎ 23 8018. Cat curiosities, posters, books and postcards plus a few items for dog lovers.
Teken aan de Wand, Huidenstraat 6, I, C3, ☎ 25 6241. Toy store for children of all ages with many hand-crafted objects: model kits, puppets, music boxes, kites and more.
1001 Kralen, Bloemgracht 38, I, B2, ☎ 24 3681. Extraordinary variety of beads.

▬ *ART GALLERIES*

d'Eendt, Spuistraat 272, I, C3, ☎ 26 5777. International and 19th– and 20th–century art (Appel, Picasso).
Espace, Leizergracht 548, I, E4, ☎ 24 0802. Dutch Figuration and contemporary Dutch painters such as Breyten, Haanstra and Roeland.
Galerie De Annex, 2ᵉ Rozendwarsstraat 3, I, B2. Works and paintings by young artists.
Galerie Paul Andriesse, Prinsengracht 116, I, B2, ☎ 23 6237. Current national and international developments in the visual arts.
Galerie Petit, N.Z. Voorburgwal 270, I, B4, ☎ 26 7507. Lyric realism in graphic art, painting, sculpture and ceramics.
Krikhaar, Spuistraat 330, I, C3, ☎ 26 7166. COBRA and Expressionist work.
Mokum, Oudezijds Voorburgwal 334, I, C4, ☎ 24 3958. Contemporary Dutch realism.
Printshop, Prinsengracht 845, I, E5, ☎ 25 1656. Permanent collection of Dutch art (Lataster, Lucebert, Dukkers, etc.). The Printshop also prints lithographs, etchings and graphic art.

Siau, Keizersgracht 267, I, C3, ☎ 26 7621. Contemporary Dutch and abstract paintings.

Steendrukkerij, Lauriergracht 80, I, D2, ☎ 24 1491. National and international contemporary graphic art. Adjacent to the exhibition room is a lithograph and screen printing studio.

Stichting De Appel, Prinseneiland 7, II, A4, ☎ 25 5651. Besides exhibitions of new art forms, De Appel has been producing interdisciplinary art projects since the mid-1980s.

▪ USEFUL VOCABULARY

English is widely spoken in Amsterdam and it is unlikely that you will have any difficulties with language. Nonetheless, efforts to speak the language are always appreciated; the following vocabulary indicates most of the useful words and phrases you may need.

Numbers, money

One	*Een*
Two	*Twee*
Three	*Drie*
Four	*Vier*
Five	*Vijf*
Six	*Zes*
Seven	*Zeven*
Eight	*Acht*
Nine	*Negen*
Ten	*Tien*
Eleven	*Elf*
Twelve	*Twaalf*
Thirteen	*Dertien*
Fourteen	*Veertien*
Fifteen	*Vijftien*
Sixteen	*Zestien*
Seventeen	*Zeventien*
Eighteen	*Achttien*
Nineteen	*Negentien*
Twenty	*Twintig*
Thirty	*Dertig*
Forty	*Veertig*
Fifty	*Vijftig*
Sixty	*Zestig*
Seventy	*Zeventig*
Eighty	*Tachtig*
Ninety	*Negentig*
One hundred	*Honderd*
Two hundred	*Tweehonderd*
One thousand	*Duizendste*
Banknote	*Bankbiljet*
Money	*Geld*
Coin	*Geldstuk*

Time and dates

Monday	*Maandag*
Tuesday	*Dinsdag*
Wednesday	*Woensdag*
Thursday	*Donderdag*
Friday	*Vrijdag*
Saturday	*Zaterdag*
Sunday	*Zondag*
January	*Januari*
February	*Februari*
March	*Maart*
April	*April*
May	*Mei*

June	*Juni*
July	*Juli*
August	*Augustus*
September	*September*
October	*Oktober*
November	*November*
December	*December*
Spring	*Lente*
Summer	*Zomer*
Autumn (fall)	*Herfst*
Winter	*Winter*
Week	*Week*
Weekday	*Werkdag*
Holiday	*Feestdag*
Hour	*Uur*
One hour	*Een uur*
One minute	*Een minuut*
Noon	*Twaalf uur*
Midnight	*Middernacht*
Weather	*Weer*
Good weather	*Mooi weer*
Wet	*Nat*
Cool	*Koel*
Cold	*Koud*
Bad weather	*Slecht weer*

Common words and phrases

Goodbye	*Tot ziens*
Good day, hello	*Goedendag*
Good evening	*Goedenavond*
Good night	*Goede nackt*
Today	*Vandaag*
Tomorrow	*Morgen*
Yesterday	*Gisteren*
Afternoon	*Middag*
Morning	*Ochtend-Morgen*
Evening	*Avond*
Careful	*Pas op*
Yes	*Ja*
Thank you	*Dank u*
No	*Nee*
Excuse me	*Pardon*
	(Neem me niet kwalijk)
If you please	*Alstublieft*
Do you speak English?	*Spreekt u Engels?*
I don't know	*Ik weet niet*
I don't understand	*Ik begrijp het niet*
I understand	*Dat begrijp ik*
What do you want?	*Wat wens u?*
I am lost	*Ik ben verdwaald*

Traveling

Boat	*Boot*
Cabin	*Kabine*
Deck	*Brug*

Ferry-boat	*Veerboot*
Port	*Haven*
Ship	*Schip*
Plane	*Vliegtuig*
Airport	*Vliegveld*
Railway	*Spoorweg*
Dining car	*Restauratiewagen*
Express train	*Exprestrein*
Fast train	*Sneltrein*
First class	*Eerste klas*
Left luggage	*Bagagedepot*
Platform	*Perron*
Porter	*Kruier*
Second class	*Tweede klas*
Sleeper	*Slaapwagen*
Slow train	*Stoptrein*
Smoking compartment	*Rookcoupé*
Station	*Station*
Sundays and holidays only	*Alleen zon- en feestdagen*
Ticket office (station)	*Loket*
Timetable (of trains)	*Spoorboekje*
Train	*Trein*
Entrance	*Ingang*
Exit	*Uitgang*
Waiting room	*Wachtkamer*
Weekdays only	*Alleen werkdagen*
Luggage	*De bagage*
Suitcase	*De koffer*
Arrival	*Aankomst*
Departure	*Vertrek*
Return	*Retour*
Ticket	*Biljet*
Customs	*Douane*
Customs office	*Douanekantoor*
Exchange office	*Wisselkantoor*
Where is the nearest ...?	*Waar is ... dichtstbijzijnde ...?*
doctor	*de ... dokter*
hotel	*het ... hotel*
garage	*de ... garage*
pharmacy	*de ... apotheek*
post office	*het ... postkantoor*
police station	*het ... politiebureau*
Is this the road for?	*Is dit de weg naar?*
Where does this road go?	*Waarheen gaat deze weg?*
Is it far from here?	*Is dat ver van hier?*
Is the service included?	*Is het bedieningsgelt inbegrepen?*
How many kilometres?	*Hoeveel kilometer?*
Can we go this way?	*Kan men hierlangs?*
Gasoline pump	*Benzinepomp*
Should I turn right or left?	*Moet ik naar links of naar rechts afslaan?*
Further	*Verder*
To be careful	*Opletten*
Downhill	*Afdaling*
Uphill	*Stijging*

Bend, corner	*Bocht*
Forest	*Bos*
Hill	*Heuvel*
Lake	*Meer*
Mountain	*Berg*
Valley	*Dal*
Village	*Dorp*
Fast	*Vlug*
Slowly	*Langzaan*

Your car

Car	*Auto*
Accelerator	*Gaspedaal*
Axle	*As, Wagenas*
Brakes	*Remmen*
Breakdown, failure	*Defect, panne*
Carburetor	*Carburator*
Clutch	*Roppeling*
Crank-shaft	*Krukas*
Garage	*Garage*
Gasoline inlet	*Benzinetoevoer*
Headlights	*Koplampen*
Jack	*Krik*
Oil pressure	*Oliedruk*
Radiator	*Radiator*
Shock absorber	*Schokbreker*
Spark plug	*Bougie*
Tyre	*Band*
To fill the radiator	*De radiator vullen*
To check the oil	*De olie controleren*
To change the wheel	*Dit wiel verwisselen*
To clean the spark plugs	*De bougies schoonmaken*
To check the tyres	*De druk op de banden controleren*

In town, shopping

Avenue	*Laan*
Bridge	*Brug*
District	*Stadswijk*
House	*Huis*
Square	*Plein*
Suburb	*Buitenwijk (Voorstad)*
Surroundings	*De omgeving*
Street	*Straat*
Town	*Stad*
Church	*Kerk*
Embassy, legation	*Ambassade, Legatie*
Town Hall	*Stadhuis*
Letter	*Brief*
Postage stamp	*Postzegel*
Post office	*Postkantoor*
Car	*Auto*
Taxi	*Taxi*
Tram	*Tram*
Bill	*Rekening*

To buy	*Kopen*
Cheap	*Goedkoop*
Check, bill	*Nota, rekening*
Expensive	*Duur*
How much?	*Hoeveel kost dat?*
To pay	*Betalen*
Price	*Prijs*
Quality	*Kwaliteit*
To sell	*Verkopen*
Store	*Winkel*

Colours

Black	*Zwart*
Colour	*Kleur*
Green	*Groen*
Red	*Rood*
White	*Wit*

At the hotel

Hotel, Inn	*Hotel*
Chambermaid	*Portier*
Bath	*Bad*
Bathroom	*Badkamer*
Bed	*Bed*
Bill	*Nota, rekening*
Blanket	*Deken*
Chair	*Stoel*
Dining room	*Eetzaal*
Elevator	*Lift*
Heating	*Verwarming*
Key	*Sleutel*
Lounge	*Salon*
Mattress	*Matras*
Pillow	*Kussen*
Room	*Kamer*
Sheet	*Laken*
Smoking room	*Rooksalon*
Stairs	*Trap*
Table	*Tafel*
Towel	*Handdoek*
Washbasin	*Wastafel*
Water	*Water*
Can you recommend a good hotel?	*Kunt u me een goed hotel aanbevelen?*
What is the price including breakfast?	*Wat is de prijs met ontbijt?*
May I see the room?	*Mag ik de kamer zien?*
Have you anything cheaper?	*Hept u iets goedkoper?*
I would like to have a ...	*Ik zou ... willen hebben*
single room	*een eenpersoonskamer*
double room with bath	*een tweenpersoonsbed met bad*
At what time is ...	*Hoe laat is ...*
breakfast?	*het ontbijt?*
lunch?	*het middageten?*
dinner?	*het avondeten?*

I want these clothes washed   *Wilt u alstublieft deze kleren in*
                                de wasdoen
Will you wake me?   *Wilt u mij wekken?*

At the restaurant

Breakfast	*Ontbijt*
Dinner	*Diner*
Lunch	*Lunch*
Menu	*Menukaart*
Restaurant	*Restaurant*
Supper	*Souper*
Waiter	*Ober*
Bottle	*Fles*
Carafe	*Karaf*
Fork	*Vork*
Glass	*Glas*
Half bottle	*Een halve fles*
Knife	*Mes*
Napkin	*Servet*
Plate	*Bord*
Spoon	*Lepel*
Beer	*Bier*
Chocolate	*Chocolade*
Coffee	*Koffie*
Dark Beer	*Donker bier*
Lager	*Licht bier*
Tea	*Thee*
Water	*Water*
Wine	*Wijn*
Bacon and eggs	*Eieren met spek*
Beef	*Rundvlees*
Bread	*Brood*
Cake	*Koek (Taart)*
Cheese	*Kaas*
Chicken	*Kip*
Cod	*Kabeljauw*
Crab	*Krab*
Cream cheese	*Roomkaas*
Duck	*Eend*
Egg	*Ei*
Fish	*Vis*
Fruit	*Fruit*
Goose	*Gans*
Halibut	*Heilbot*
Herring	*Haring*
Hors-d'oeuvre	*Hors-d'oeuvre*
Lobster	*Kreeft*
Mackerel	*Makreel*
Meat	*Vlees*
Mushrooms	*Champignons*
Mustard	*Mosterd*
Mutton	*Schapevlees*
Pepper	*Peper*
Pork	*Varkensvlees*
Potatoes	*Aardappelen*
Salad	*Sla*
Salmon	*Zalm*

Salt	*Zout*
Sardines	*Sardientjes*
Shrimp	*Garnalen*
Sugar	*Suiker*
Tomatoes	*Tomaten*
Trout	*Forel*
Turbot	*Tarbot*
Veal	*Kalfsvlees*
Vegetables	*Groente*
Less	*Minder*
A little	*Weinig*
More, another	*Meer, nog eens*
Not enough	*Niet voldoende*
May I see the menu?	*Mag ik de spijskaart zien?*
What do you recommend?	*Wat kunt u aanbevelen?*
Please give us some . . .	*Geeft u ons wat . . .*
May I have the check, please?	*Mag ik de rekening, alstublieft?*
Is the tip included?	*Is de bediening inbegrepen?*
Thank you, it was very good	*Dank u, het was een uitstekende maaltijd.*

▬ SUGGESTED READING

Art and Architecture

Clark, Kenneth. *An Introduction to Rembrandt* (Harper & Row, 1979).

Fromentin, Eugene. *The Masters of Past Time: Dutch and Flemish Painting from Van Eyck to Rembrandt* (Cornell, 1981).

Fuchs, R.H. *Dutch Painting* (Thames & Hudson, 1985).

Panofsky, E. *Early Netherlandish Painting: Its Origins and Character* (Harper & Row, 1971).

Rosenburg, Jakob. *Dutch Art and Architecture* (Penguin, 1972).

Schapiro, Meyer. *Van Gogh* (Abrams, 1984).

Stone, Irving, ed. *Dear Theo: The Autobiography of Vincent Van Gogh* (Doubleday, 1969).

History and Background

Bailey, Anthony. *Rembrandt's House* (Houghton Mifflin, 1978).

Burnchurch, R. *An Outline of Dutch History* (Heinemann, 1982).

Colijn, Helen. *Of Dutch Ways* (Barnes & Noble, 1984).

Cotterell, Geoffrey. *Amsterdam: The Life of a City* (Little Brown, 1973).

Hugget, Frank. E. *The Modern Netherlands* (Praeger, 1971).

Huizinga, Johan. *The Waning of the Middle Ages* (St. Martin's, 1984).

Kossman, E.H. *The Low Countries, 1780-1940* (Oxford, 1978).

Multatuli (pseud.) *Max Havelaar: Of the Coffee Auctions of the Dutch Trading Company* (University of Massachusetts Press, 1982).

Schama, Simon. *The Embarrassment of Riches: An Interpretation of Dutch Culture in the Golden Age* (Knopf, 1987).

Stoutenbeek, Jan et al. *A Guide to Jewish Amsterdam* (Hermon, 1985).

Literature

Camus, Albert. *The Fall* (Knopf, 1957).

Dumas, Alexander. *The Black Tulip* (Dutton, 1961).

Frank, Anne. *The Diary of a Young Girl* (Washington Square Press, 1987).

Hartog, Jan de. *The Little Ark* (Atheneum, 1970).

MacLean, Alistair. *Floodgate* (Doubleday, 1984).

Mulisch, Harry. *The Assault* (Pantheon, 1985).

Oberski, Jona. *Childhood* (NAL, 1984).

Weterling, Janwillen van de. *The Streetbird* (Putnam, 1983).

Wolkers, Jan. *Turkish Delight* (Marion Boyars, 1983).

INDEX

Access, 15-16
Accommodation, 19
  in Amsterdam, 117-119
  in Edam, 106
  in Haarlem, 112-113
  in Monnickendam, 102
  in Muiden, 113
  in Naarden, 116
  in Volendam, 105
Airlines, 19
Alechinsky, Pierre, 94, 96
Allard Pierson Museum, 98-99
Amstelkring Museum, 62-63
Amsterdam Tourist Bureau, 35
Amsterdams Historich Museum, *see* **Historical Museum**
Anabaptism, 38-39
Andriessen, Mari, 73
Anne Frank House, 68-69
Antiques, 125
Appel, Karel, 94, 96, 111, 126
Architecture
  Amsterdam School of, 81-84
  see also 'Urban Planning'
Art
  contemporary, 53-54
  galleries, 126-127
  see also 'Museums'
Artis Museum-Zoo, 99-100
Auction houses, 125

Banks, 20
Begijnhof, 38, 65
Berlage, Petrus, 64
Berlage Bridge, 84
Bible Museum, 70
Bicycle, 26, 33, 52
Boat, 27, 28
Bol, Ferdinand, 89, 97

Bookshops, 58, 125
Botanical Gardens, 100
Breitner, George Henrik, 87
Brown cafés *see* **Cafés and bars**
Bruegel the Elder, 88
Budget, 18
Bus
  in Amsterdam, 28
  to Amsterdam, 16
Business hours, 19-20

Cafés and bars, 26, 121-122
Calvinism, 39
Campen, Jacob van, 56, 61, 72, 85, 96
Campgrounds, 119
Car
  rental, 28
  see also 'Driving'
Carnival, 22
Catholicism, 38-39, 62
Centraal Station, 86
Chagall, Marc, 94, 95
Cheese, 25, 105
  farm, 102
Churches
  clandestine, 62-63, 65
  see also proper names
Claes Claeszhofje, 78-79
Climate, 15
Clothing stores, 125
COBRA, 94, 96, 111, 126
Comenius (Jan Amos Komensky), 115
Concertgebouw, 22, 45, 53
Constant, 96
Consulates, *see* **Embassies and consulates**
Corneille, 96
Cornelisz van Haarlem, Cornelis, 88, 110

Cornelisz van Oostasanen, Jacob, 88
Crafts, 125
Credit cards, 18
Cuijpers, Josephus Hubertus, 64
Currency exchange, 20
Customs, 16-17
Cuyp, Albert, 89
Cuypers, Petrus J., 86

Economy, 49-50
Edam, 105-106
Eigenhaard Building Cooperative, 83-84
Electricity, 20
Embassies and consulates
  Dutch, abroad, 18
  foreign, in Netherlands, 21
Emergencies, 21
Entertainment, 21-22, 122-124
Epen, J.C. van, 84

Dam, The, 55-58
Damrak, 55, 64-65
Dance, 22, 122
De Dageraad Building Cooperative, 82-83
Dekker Douwes, Eduard, *see* **Multatuli**
De Kleine Komedie, 22
De Kooning, Willem, 93, 95
Department stores, 124
Descartes, René, 66, 68
De Stijl, 94, 95
Diamond trade, 32, 39, 45, 46, 126
Discotheques, 123
Doesburg, Theo van, 94, 95
Dortsman, Adriaan, 71
Dotremont, Christian, 96
Driegrachtenhuis, *see* **House of the Three Canals**
Driving
  in Amsterdam, 27-28
  licence and insurance, 160
  to Amsterdam, 16
Drugs, 48, 53
Dubuffet, Jean, 93
Dürer, Albrecht, 86
Dutch East and West India Companies, 39, 42, 43, 44, 61, 80

Festivals, *see* **Holidays**
Film, 54
Fishing, 53
Flower
  markets, 33, 66
  Parade, 24
  trade, 108-109
Fodor Museum, 70-71
Food and Drink, 24-26, 126
  see also 'Restaurants'
Frank, Anne, 68
Frans Hals Museum, 108-110-111

Gauguin, Paul, 90, 91, 92
Geertgen tot Sint Jans, 87, 109
Gelder, Aert de, 89
Gildewart, 94, 95
Glossary, 128-133
Goltzius, Hendrik, 112
Goyen, Jan van, 89
Groot, Kees de, 54
Gym, 33

East Indies, 46, 62
  see also 'Dutch East and West India Companies'

Haarlem, 45, 101, 107-113

Haarlem School of Painting, 109
Haitink, Bernard, 53
Hals, Frans, 89, 109, 111
  see also 'Frans Hals Museum'
Hart, Martin 't, 54
Heemskerck, Maerten van, 110
Herenmarkt, 80
Herring, 22, 38
Historical Museum, 65, 96-98
Holidays, 22-24
Holland Festival, 24
Hop, Jacob, 71
Hortus Botanicus, *see* **University Botanical Gardens**
Hospitals, 21
Hostels, 119
Hotels
  classification, 117
  see also 'Accommodation'
House of the Three Canals, 58
Housing, 50-52
Huguenots, 41, 67, 77, 112

Ice skating, 34
Immigration, 52-53, 67
Israel, Manasse ben, 73
Israëls, Isaac, 87, 111

Jewelry, 126
Jewish
  Historical Museum, 73
  quarter, 40, 60, 72-74
Jews, 39, 45-46, 67, 68
Jonas Daniel Meijerplein, 45, 73
Joods Historich Museum, *see* **Jewish Historical Museum**
Jordaan, 67, 77-79, 124
  Festival, 24
Jorn, Asger, 96

Katwoude, 102
Keyser, Hendrik de, 66, 68, 70, 76, 79, 97
Keyser, Pieter de, 96
Keyser, Thomas de, 63
Keyser, Willem de, 57
Klerk, Michel de, 81, 82, 83, 84
Koninginnedag, 23-24
Koninklijk Paleis, *see* **Royal Palace**
Kramer, Pieter, 81, 82, 84
Krop, Hildo, 81, 82, 83

Language, 29
  see also **Glossary**
Lastman, Pieter, 75
Lataster, Ger, 53, 126
Leck, Bart van der, 95
Leyden, Lucas van, 88, 112
Literature
  contemporary, 54
  Renaissance, 40
  see also authors' proper names
Lucebert, 95, 126

Madame Tussaud's Museum, 65
Maes, Nicolaes, 89
Malevitch, 94, 95
Mander, Karel van, 109, 111
Marken, 101, 102-104
Markets, 32-33, 124-125
  antique, 79
  bird, 79
  clothing, 79
  flea, 73, 79
Master of Alkmaar, Anonymous, 87
Matisse, Henri, 94
Media, 29-30
Medical care, 21
Meitner, Richard, 54
Mint Tower, 55, 66
Mondrian, Piet, 94, 95

Money, 17-18
  see also 'Currency exchange'
Monnickendam, 101-102
Montelbaan Tower (Montelbaanstoren), 55, 60-61
Moses and Aaron Church, 73-74
Mostaert, Jan, 87
Muiden, 101
Muiden Castle, 113
Muiderpoort, 55
Mulisch, Harry, 54
Multatuli, 44, 79
Munttoren, see Mint Tower
Multi-media
  art, 54
  centres, 123-124
Museums, 85-100
see also proper names
Music, 22, 122-124
Muziektheater, 22, 72, 122

Naarden, 101, 115-116
Naarderbos, 115
Napoleon Bonaparte, 44
Napoleon, Louis, 44, 56, 85
Nederlands Scheepvaart Museum, see Netherlands Maritime Museum
Netherland Board of Tourism, 18
Netherlands Maritime Museum, 61-62
Newspapers, 29-30
New Church, 55, 56-58
Nieuwekerk, see New Church
Nieuwmarkt, 51, 60
Nightlife, 122-124
Noorderkerk, 79
Nooteboom, Cees, 54

Old Church, 22-23, 38, 55, 63-64
Ostade, Adriaen van, 89

Ouborg, Pieter, 94
Oude Kerk, see Old Church

Parking lots, 28
Passport, 16
Pietersz, Pieter, 88, 110
Plane, 15
Portuguese Synagogue, 73
Post, 31-32
Potter, Paulus, 89
Prinseneiland, 80
Proeflokaal, see Cafés and bars
Protestantism, 39, 41, 64
Provos, 47, 48, 52, 60, 65

Rademakers, Fons, 54
Radio, 30
Red-light district, 62, 64
Reformation, 38-39, 62
  see also 'Protestantism'
Regulierspoort, see Mint Tower
Rembrandt, 40, 60, 64, 65, 68, 73, 74, 75, 88, 89, 112
Rembrandt's House, 75
Restaurants, 25, 117
  classification, 117
  in Amsterdam, 119-121
  in Edam, 107
  in Haarlem, 113
  in Monnickendam, 102
  in Muiden, 113
  in Naarden, 116
  in Volendam, 105
  see also 'Food and drink'
Rijksmuseum, 45, 85-89
Ruisdael, Jacob van, 89, 97, 109
Royal Palace, 56, 85
Rutpers, G.J., 84

Safety, 32
St Antony's Gate, *see* Waag, The
St Nicholas
  churches dedicated to, 63
  Day, 24
  Parade, 24
Schiphol Airport, 16, 50
Schreierstoren, *see* Weeper's Tower
Schuilkerken, *see* Churches, clandestine
Scorel, Jan van, 88
Seghers, Hercules, 86
Shipbuilding industry, 38
Shopping, 32-33, 124-126
Siehuis, Jan, 53
Sint Andrieshof, 78
Sint Antoniespoort, *see* Waag, The
Sluyters, Jan, 111
Spinoza, Baruch, 40, 41
Sports, 33-34
Squatter movement, 50-51
Stadsschouwburg, 21, 45, 122
Staets, Hendrik, 79
Stedelijk Museum, 93-96
Steen, Jan, 89
Stille Omgang, 22-23
Stopera, *see* Muziektheater
Stuyvesant, Peter, 80
Subway, 28, 60
Suriname, 47
  immigrants from, 52
Swimming pools, 34
Synagogues, 73

Telephone, 34
Television, 30
Teyler Museum, 111-112
Teyler's Almshouse, 114
Theatre, 21-22, 122
  see also proper names
Theatre Carré, 21, 122
Theatre de Ebgelbak, 21
Theatre Museum, 70
Time, 34
Tipping, 34
Torenburg, 65
Tourist information, 35

Tours, 33
Train, 16
Tram, 28
Transportation
  in Amsterdam, 26-29
  to Amsterdam, 15-16
Treaty of Munster, 40
Trip brothers, 58-59
Troost, Cornelis, 87
Troostwijk, Wouter van, 87
Tropenmuseum, *see* Tropical Museum
Tropical Museum, 99
Tulips, 108-109

University Botanical Gardens, 100
Urban planning, 50-52, 76, 77
  see also 'Architecture'

Vaccinations, 16
Valckert, W.J. van den, 89
Van Gogh, Vincent, 13, 89-93, 94
Van Gogh Museum, 89-93
Van Loon Museum, 71
Verhoeven, Paul, 54
Vermeer, Jan, 89
Video, *see* Film
Visserplein, 72
VOCA, 61, 106
  see also 'Dutch East and West India Companies'
Voegingeweij, Leo, 54
Volendam, 101, 104-105
Vondel, Joost van den, 40, 58, 61, 96
Vondelpark, 24, 95-96

Waag, The, 55, 60
Walloon Church, 112
Waterlooplein, 51, 72
Weepers' Tower, 55, 62
Westerkerk, *see* **Western**
Church
Westermarkt, 40
Western Church, 68, 72, 77
Wezel, Adriaen van, 89
Willet Holthuysen Museum,
71-72
World War II, 45-46

Zoo, 99-100
Zuiderkerk, 76
Zuiderzee, 101, 103, 104